To Save a Lady

ARDEN STEWART

Copyright © 2022 Arden Stewart

All rights reserved. No part of this book may be reproduced or used in any manner without written permission of the copyright owner except for the use of quotations in a book review.

First Edition

Hardback: 979-8-9859798-2-4

DEDICATION

This book is first dedicated to Dr. Olga "Candy" Lawson.

Also dedicated to my parents, Edna and Earl Stewart, who supported me in anything I wanted to try, and my wonderful Aunt Dora Ketchum. Also some special friends Sophronia Rein and Annis Rae Reid for their support.

I also want to acknowledge my graphic designer Emily Eaton for her patience and expertise in formatting and editing my book.

Thanks also to my friend Maura Hudson for her seductive picture of The Lady that I used as the book cover picture.

SPECIAL THANKS

Special thanks to Lorraine Trudeau Achee in customer service, who advocated for me, and Harriet Kensler, vice president, both of what was then Hibernia National Bank St. Charles branch. I learned recently from Lorraine, though I was qualified for a loan for some interim financing I needed, I was going to be denied on the basis that I was a single woman. Ms. Kensler would have none of that. I got the loan. This was in the late 60's. Harriet Kensler and Lorraine Achee fought for fairness in financing for women.

Special thanks to my old friend Betsy Swanson for her advice and the suggestion to emphasize the major elements of my house using the colors of the roof slate.

Betsy Swanson is a well-known historian and photographer. She has published books and papers on local architecture and important historic forts. Her photographs are a major contribution to many local architectural publications.

Special thanks to Lyle Columbo, a friend and former resident of The Lady, for help in researching information I needed.

SPECIAL THANKS

Special thanks to Mark Marley for editing large portions of *To Save a Lady*.

Special thanks to Mimi Landry for naming the house ghost spirit, naming all my pets, and for just being Mimi. Mimi was my first tenant and lived in the house for almost 30 years before buying her own house.

Special thanks to Scott Taranto, owner of New Orleans Millworks, which specializes in historic architectural repair and reproduction. Thank you, Scott, for perfectly reproducing the many different pieces of gingerbread I needed to repair The Lady.

FOREWORD

I did not only write this book, I lived it.

I tried to tell a simple story of how and what I did to save a deteriorating grand old house I named The Lady. The Lady lived at 4032 Prytania, corner of Prytania and Marengo, in New Orleans, Louisiana. However, I found I sometimes became interested in details of the process. A lot of New Orleanians spend a good part of their time and money on their homes. Most are trying to restore a typical style of New Orleans house. These people may find my digressions and details interesting and familiar.

I acquired The Lady in 1967. I worked on her for 50-plus years and the saving repairs are ongoing. I made repairs when I had the money. It was slow going. I would stay and watch as the repairs were made. Most of the workman would explain the what and how of the repairs. As a result, I learned a lot about sheetrock, carpentry, roofing, and plumbing.

TABLE OF CONTENTS

Chapter 1	9	The Lady
Chapter 2	27	History of Property
Chapter 3	44	Outside Architecture and Gingerbread
Chapter 4	74	Changes After 1919 Sale
Chapter 5	82	Interior Changes
Chapter 5.1	83	First Floor
Chapter 5.2	100	Second Floor
Chapter 5.3	115	Third Floor
Chapter 6	118	Damage to Exterior
Chapter 6.1	119	Turret Repair
Chapter 6.2	128	Roof
Chapter 6.3	141	Gutters
Chapter 6.4	144	Cedar Scales
Chapter 6.5	149	Porch Support, Brickwork, and Grates
Chapter 6.6	154	Porch Floor
Chapter 6.7	164	Porch Wall and Ceilings
Chapter 6.8	173	Porch Railings

TABLE OF CONTENTS

Chapter 7	178	Interesting Things About The Lady
Chapter 8	193	A House and a Home
Chapter 8.1	194	The Flaspollers
Chapter 8.2	196	Tenants Through the Years
Chapter 8.3	210	Is The Lady Haunted?
Chapter 9	215	Of Interest to Some
Chapter 9.1	216	The Flaspoller Family
Chapter 9.2	231	Costs
Chapter 9.3	238	Workmen Helped Save The Lady

CHAPTER 1

The Lady

Chapter 1: The Lady

The house at 4032 Prytania was contracted to be built by a woman, Mrs. Anna Wilhelmina Potthorst Flaspoller, in 1893. The builder's name was Antoine Lagmann, and the architect was William Fitzner.

This drawing of The Lady is by Jane Brewster. She used some old pictures to create this drawing. I believe this truly represents The Lady as she was originally built.

Chapter 1: The Lady

When I purchased The Lady in 1967, she just looked miserable. There were trees and large oleander plants surrounding and practically obscuring the house. Junk cars were parked on the Marengo Street side and laundry could be seen flapping in the breeze on the second floor porch. The house had been cut up into 14 apartments: A, B, C, D, E, F, G, H, I, J, K, L, M, and N.

Below is a picture of the Lady from 1943 when it was sold. It shows many trees obstructing the view of the house.

I bought The Lady in 1967. I was 29 at the time and could only see the beauty that was once there. My father asked me why I didn't buy a nice double, but then he said I was young enough to make a mistake. I took that as encouragement.

Chapter 1: The Lady

This is a picture of The Lady that I found from 1915. Although there are a lot of trees, we are able to see some useful parts to the house that are now gone. Most important are the first and second floor railings on the Marengo Street side, which show the symmetry of the house.

RESIDENCE OF MISS FLASPOLLER
4032 Prytania Street

Painted with *Hammer Strictly Pure White Lead* by Mr. Philip Hasselbeck, 2022 Annunciation street, whose satisfactory work is shown in the above residence as well as many others throughout the city, *M. AUGUSTIN, 323 Baronne St.*, is the Southern Distributor, Hammer White Lead Company.

Picture of The Lady 9/19/1915 with ad for white lead paint. As both Flaspoller parents by then were deceased, The Lady was then owned by daughter Miss Caroline Flaspoller and her sister Mrs. Bertha Flaspoller Drott, divorced wife of William Drott.

Chapter 1: The Lady

In 1977, I had a tenant, Cornelius "Lee" Alig. He was a graduate student at Tulane University in New Orleans in the architecture department. Lee wrote a paper on New Orleans architecture and included 4032 in his research.

It was because of Lee's research, which included The Lady, that I became interested in its history.

The following pictures, taken by photographer Ben VanDusen in 1977, show Lee and various architectural parts of The Lady.

Lee Alig on the roof. Photographs by Ben VanDusen, 1977.

As part of his research, Lee also found and contacted relatives of the original owners. One of the relatives, a granddaughter of the Flaspollers, was Mrs. West (originally Estelle Flaspoller). She gave Lee important information about what she remembered about The Lady. She also gave Lee some pictures. These were part of what was used by Jane Brewster to draw and show what the house looked like when owned by the Flaspollers.

Happy Times

At one time the house was happy. There were children, a solarium with beautiful plants, people who cared about the house and cared about each other. There was a music room where there was lots of laughter and happy times.

Here are two examples of happy times:

Bertha Drott's Christmas Dance
Daily Picayune, December 30, 1900

Among the beautiful Christmas celebrations of the week was the dance given Thursday evening by Miss Bertha Drott in honor of her young college friends, at the residence of her grandmother, Mrs. Flaspoller. The decorations were most artistic, consisting of the typical Christmas holly festooned with crimson ribbons above the windows and trailing over the curtains. Garlands of the bright red berries and glossy green leaves were wreathed about the chandeliers and pictures and draped about the walls. Palms and ferns were grouped about the halls and library, and crimson carnations banked the mantels and were arranged in vases throughout the house. The table decorations were of pink roses and silver candelabra holding pink waxen candles. Rose-colored ribbons were brought from the chandeliers to the four corners of the board, where they were tied in large bow-knots. The pretty young hostess, gowned in pink chiffon, was assisted in receiving by Miss Caroline Flaspoller and Miss Hazel Conniff.

Chapter 1: The Lady

On 11/19/1905, a granddaughter of Mrs. Anna Flaspoller was married. Mrs Bertha Flaspoller Drott issued invitations to the marriage of her daughter, Bertha, to Mr. John Robinson Conniff on November 29 ,1905, at St. George's Church with a reception at the home of the bride, 4032 Prytania.

Chapter 1: The Lady

The following pictures, given to Lee by Mrs. West (formerly Estelle Flaspoller, a granddaughter), show some of the exterior of the house as it was when owned by the Flaspollers. These pictures were used by Jane Brewster to create the rendering of the original structure of The Lady.

To the right of the curved porch was an enclosed porch which was a solarium

Victorians were very interested in gardens and plants.

Inside solarium

Chapter 1: The Lady

Marengo side of the house showing the side entrance, which was on the right end of the solarium.

To the right of the side entrance shows a garden full of plants. The windows in the background are part of the inside dining area.

Chapter 1: The Lady

Outside of the yard in front of the iron fence and the side entrance are Estelle and Tuttle, grandchildren of Mrs. Anna Flaspoller. Their father was H. H. Flaspoller.

I didn't realize until later that this was the Estelle, now Mrs. West, that Lee had spoken to and who had been so helpful. Estelle Flaspoller married William A. West, Jr. in 1923. One of their children was Roger Blake West. He later became a judge. I met Judge and Mrs. Willey West when they visited The Lady. Mrs. Blake West wrote me a nice letter thanking me for showing them what I was doing to restore and repair The Lady.

Chapter 1: The Lady

This is a picture of the cistern. It was in the back yard and used to catch water from the rain.

Clean drinking water had always been a problem. Wells could not be used, as when digging even a few feet into the ground, you would hit spongy bogs. To provide clean water, residents relied on cisterns. These were massive wood or iron cylinders that were open on the top for collecting rainwater. However, mosquitoes laid their eggs in the open tanks. There were many deaths from Yellow Fever.

The last Yellow Fever epidemic was in 1905. This was the year doctors working at Walter Reed Hospital discovered the link between mosquitoes and Yellow Fever.

It was at this time it was ordered that all standing water be covered.

When I bought The Lady, the cistern body was gone. What was left was a circle of a brick wall filled with soil with a tree planted in the center. I removed the soil and the tree. The picture shows the construction of the base of the cistern.

I had the inner brick removed and had the wall made waterproof to make into a pond.

The finished pond, complete with goldfish, much to the delight of my dog Gita.

Chapter 1: The Lady

The swing set picture was taken in the front yard facing Prytania.

The house across the street on the left was built by Mrs. Flaspoller in 1892. She acquired the property May 16, 1887. This is probably where she lived while The Lady was being built. Her son and his family later lived in it for a time while waiting for his house at 5308 Prytania to be built.

In 1907, The Lady's first bathroom was added. It was supported by brackets and posts and had The Lady's first plumbing. There had likely been no good place for it in the original house.

Chapter 1: The Lady

In 1893, the city leaders began planning for a system to provide drainage, drinking water, water for fire protection, and a sanitary sewerage system.

In 1896, the New Orleans Drainage Commission was organized to carry out a master drainage plan that had been developed for the city.

Three years later in 1899, the Sewerage and Water Board was authorized by the Louisiana Legislature to construct and maintain a water treatment and distribution system and a sanitary sewerage system in New Orleans.

In 1903, the Drainage Commission and the Sewerage and Water Board merged under one agency that was called the Sewerage and Water Board.

Even though the house was built in 1893, the first record I have of indoor plumbing was in 1907.

Below is a copy of the plumbing application to the Sewerage and Water Board on November 29, 1907. Charlton Bros., master plumbers on Magazine St., completed the work. The work was to be done on the river side of Prytania St., No. 4032. The permit was applied for by Mrs. B. H. Flaspoller.

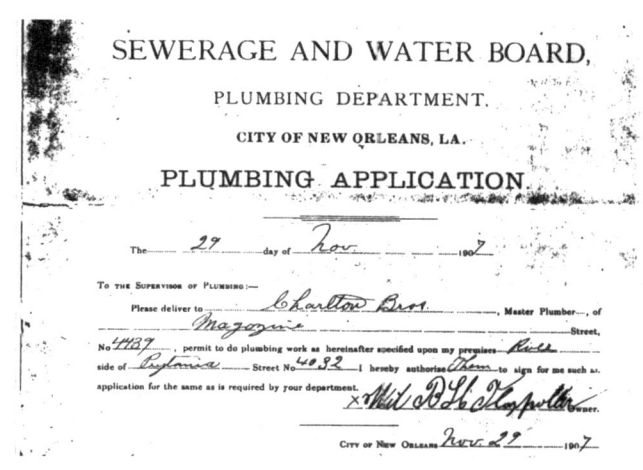

Fixtures ordered—one water closet-style Gen. Douglas Record with separate tank, one wash bowl, one bathtub

I went online to see what a Gen. Douglas toilet looked like. I found out the name of the toilet was actually John Douglas, not Gen. as listed on the old record.

Most people think the slang term "going to the John" came from the John Douglas Co., which marketed toilets that had the name John on them. Some think the word came from the word "jakes" or "jacks," which were medieval English terms for a place to go to the bathroom.

Water closet style probably meant with wall-hung water tank.

This is how an application for plumbing would look at this time.

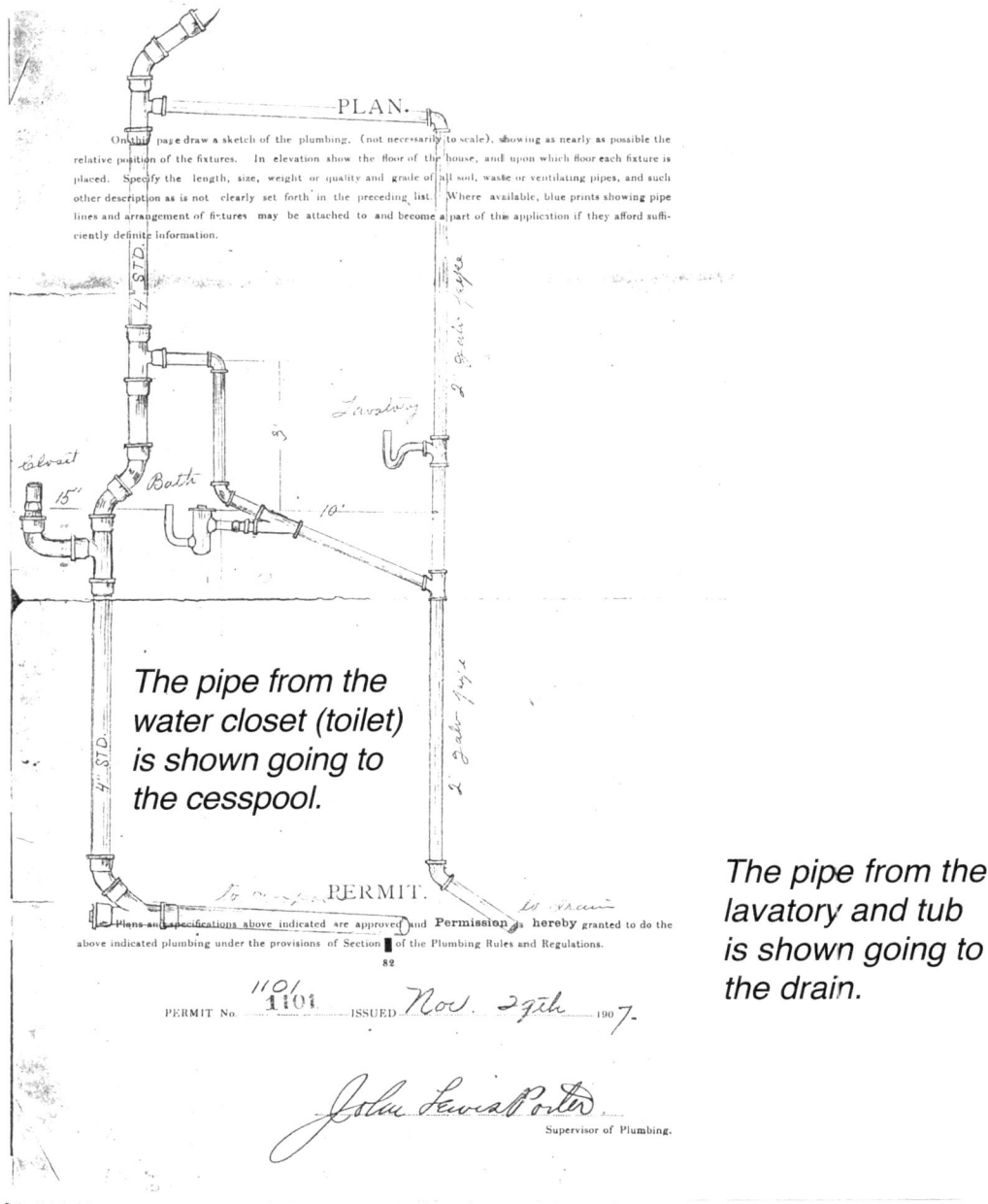

The pipe from the water closet (toilet) is shown going to the cesspool.

The pipe from the lavatory and tub is shown going to the drain.

This is what is written on the drawing: On this page draw a sketch of the plumbing, (not necessarily to scale), showing as nearly as possible the relative position of the fixtures. In elevation show the floor of the house, and upon which floor each fixture is placed. Specify the length, size, weight or quality and grade of all soil, waste or ventilating pipes, and such other description as is not clearly set forth in the preceding list. Where available, blue prints showing pipe lines and arrangement of fixtures may be attached to and become a part of this application if they afford sufficiently definite information.

CHAPTER 2

History of Property

Chapter 2: History of Property

Our property of interest was part of the Cottage Plantation. 1856 was the first specific mention of a part of the Cottage Plantation being surveyed and split up. The survey done in 1863 shows Square #51 (later #337), which was comprised of 18 lots.

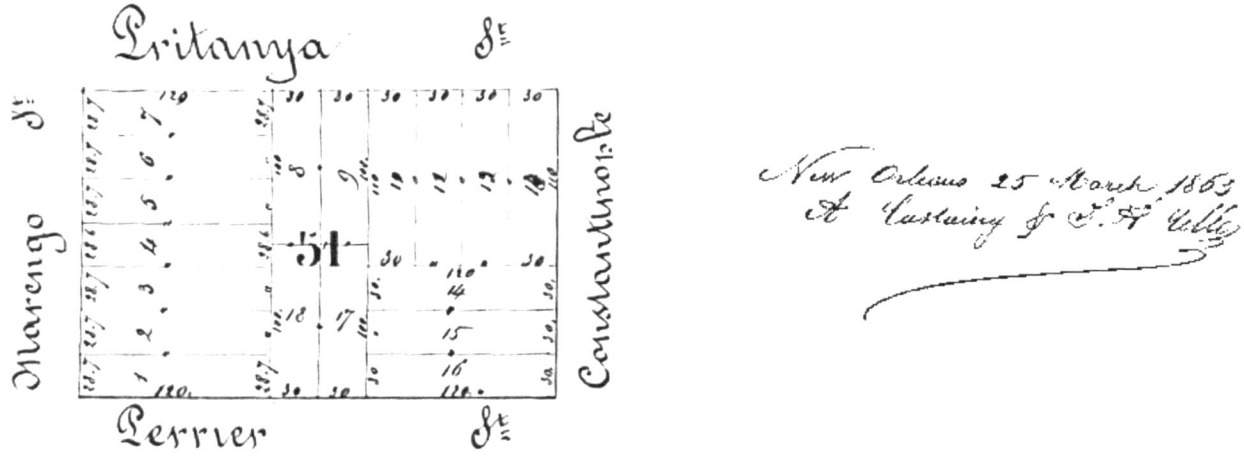

Prytania St.

Marengo St. — **Constantinople St.**

Perrier St.

On April 16, 1867, George Hawkins sold to Bernard H. Flaspoller Lots 5, 6, and 7, forming the corner of Prytania and Marengo for $1,350.00 (shown here as Lot 7).

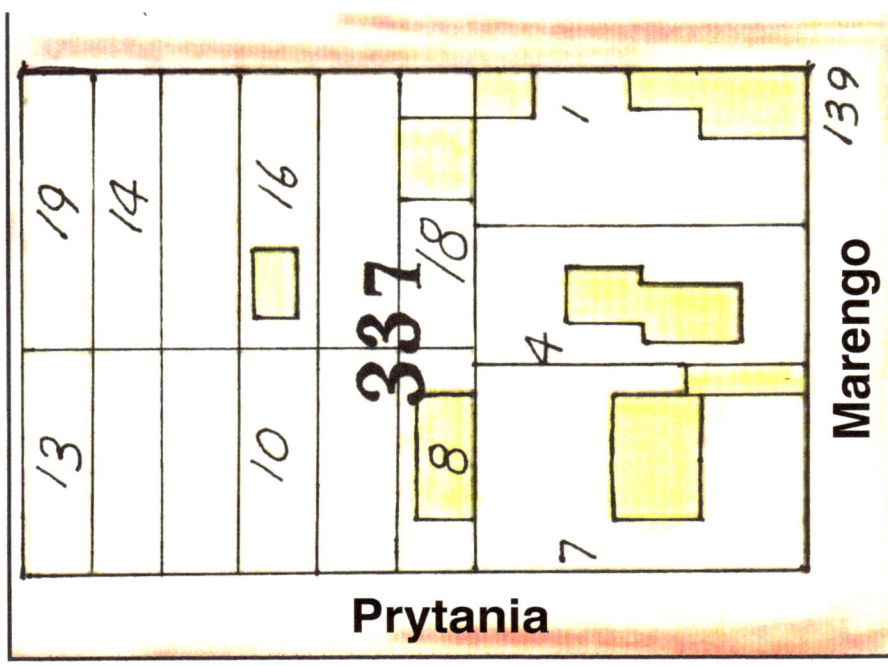

Robinson's Atlas of the City of New Orleans, *published in 1883 but compiled in 1875, shows a large square building on the southeast corner of Prytania and Marengo in Lot 7*

The city directory listings show that a house was located at the corner of Prytania and Marengo as early as 1873 and was a residence for B. H. Flaspoller. It was also listed as his residence in 1874 and 1875.

An interesting thing is that the location of the residence given in 1873 and 1874 is "Marengo corner Prytania," but from 1875 on, it was given as "Prytania corner Marengo."

Bernard H. Flaspoller died on April 5, 1886, at Blount Springs, Alabama where he had gone for his health. The funeral took place at his late residence, Marengo and Prytania Sts.

In 1891, the city directory listed August H. & H. C. and Anna, widow, residing at Prytania and Marengo.

Chapter 2: History of Property

On December 21, 1892, Mrs. Bernard H. Flaspoller and Antoine Lagmann entered into a contract to build The Lady.

The following are portions of the building contract. The building contract only tells that a house was to be built, the price, and when it would be completed. The plans for building The Lady were probably kept by the architect. I was not able to find a copy.

The plot or portion of land belonging to Mrs. Anna Flaspoller in the 6th District was in the square bounded by Prytania, Marengo, Perrier and Constantinople. It measured 176', more or less, front on Prytania and 100' in depth between parallel lines and front on Marengo.

Prytania St.

| Marengo St. | | | Constantinople St. |

(Diagram of lot layout: Lots 1–7 along Marengo St., Lots 8, 9, 17, 18 in the middle, Lots 10–16 along Constantinople St. Lots 4, 5, 6, 7, 8, and 9 are highlighted.)

Perrier St.

The 100 feet on Marengo was made up of Lots 5, 6, and 7 and half of Lot 4. This half was purchased by B. H. Flaspoller in 1884 for $210.00. All of these lots were 120 feet in depth.

Upon Mrs. Flaspoller's death in 1910, Lots 8, 9, and 10 were listed among her property owned. In the building contract of 1892, the property was listed as being size 176', more or less, on Prytania and 100' on Marengo, which must have included 8 and 9.

Contract Continues

An order to remove buildings, carriage house, outhouses, cistern, and other appurtenances from their present location to a new location was shown on a plan called *Situation Plan*. I do not have a copy of this *Situation Plan*.

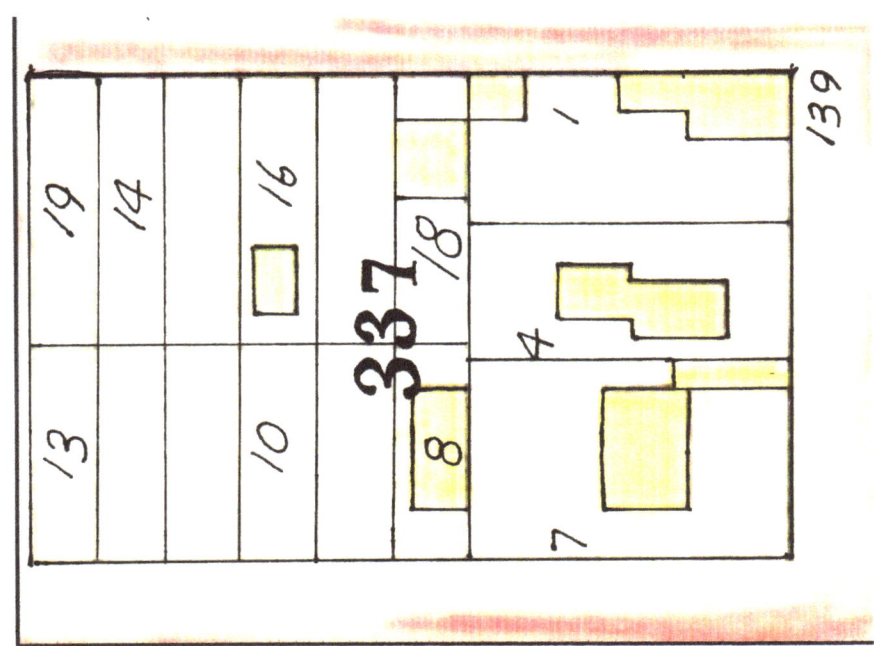

This map is from 1875 and the building contract is from 1892. The buildings shown on Lot 4 and Lot 8 might not have been the ones referred to in the contract.

The removal and the re-erecting were done according to the *Removal Plan*. I do not have a copy of this *Removal Plan*.

These structures were to be moved further down Prytania, which would have a 61' front on Prytania with a depth of 100'. The 114' 6" that remained on the front left on Prytania to the corner was where The Lady was built.

This removal, restoration, and alterations of the moved structures were to be completed on or before March 1893, for the sum of $1,800.00.

The contract between Mrs. Anna Flaspoller and the builder, Mr. Antoine Lagmann, continues:

...and then build a two story frame dwelling house and other improvements and appurtenances to be completed prior to July 1, 1893, for Mrs. Flaspoller for a cost of $13,445.00.

The site on which both of these tasks were to be done measured 176' on Prytania by 100' depth on Marengo.

The whole building contract is included in a separate chapter for those who are interested.

Lot 7 was originally 120' on Prytania, but only 114.6' was used to build The Lady. The other 5.6' was added to Lots 8, 9, and 10 and later divided into 2 lots, approximately 47. 8' each.

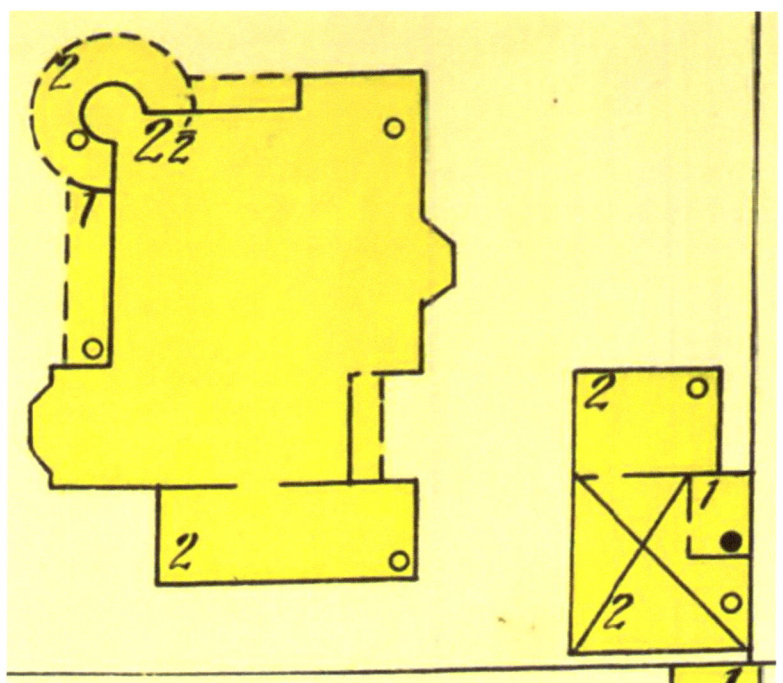

Map in 1893 shows house with two story Carriage House. Lot size is 114.6' on Prytania by 100' on Marengo.

Mrs. B. H. Flaspoller

The unexpected death of Mrs. B. H. Flaspoller yesterday forenoon at her home, on Prytania and Marengo Streets, caused much genuine sorrow among her numerous friends throughout the city. Mrs. Flaspoller, though advanced in years, was a woman of remarkable vigor, and was an active worker of St. George's Episcopal Church, of the German Protestant Orphan Asylum and of the German Home for the Aged and Infirm.

She was a member of the board of managers of both the last named institutions for many years, and was the treasurer of the German Home since its organization, twenty-five years ago. Her presence and help will be greatly missed by these organizations and the many other worthy causes she so generously assisted.

She leaves to mourn her two sons, August H. and Henry Flaspoller, of the wholesale grocery firm of B. H. Flaspoller's Sons, founded by her husband and herself more than fifty years ago. She also leaves two daughters, Mrs. B. F. Drott and Miss Carrie Flaspoller, numerous grandchildren and a great-grandchild.

The funeral will take place this afternoon at 4 o'clock and Rev. Byron Holley, of St. George's, will officiate.

I could not find the cause of Mrs. Anna Flaspoller's death, but I found this in the newspaper:

Mrs. Henry H. Flaspoller arrived last evening from Covington, La., called here by the sudden death of her mother-in-law, Mrs. B. H. Flaspoller, who passed away yesterday, after three days of intense suffering.

Mrs. Anna Wilhelmina Potthorst Flaspoller died in May, 1910, at the age of 70.

Since The Lady was built in 1893, Mrs. Flaspoller's age when she built The Lady would have been 53. The Lady was in the Flaspoller family for 26 years, from 1893 until 1919.

She was a feisty lady

12/20/1905 - Interfering with Health Officer
From the fever times last summer, Mrs. Albrecht and Mrs. Flaspoller objected to Health Officers fumigating their house, as it would damage a piano. It was alleged they cursed, abused him, and interfered with him as to delay fumigating the premises.

1910 In the succession of Mrs. Anna Wilhelmina Potthorst Flaspoller, widow of Bernard H. Flaspoller, she leaves everything to her four children.
Mrs. Bertha Ann Flaspoller, divorced wife of William Drott
August H. Flaspoller
Miss Caroline Anna Flaspoller
Henry H. Flaspoller

Chapter 2: History of Property

The property listed in Mrs. Anna Flaspoller's succession consisted of The Lady and eight other pieces of property. Each of her children took two pieces of the eight but co-owned The Lady.

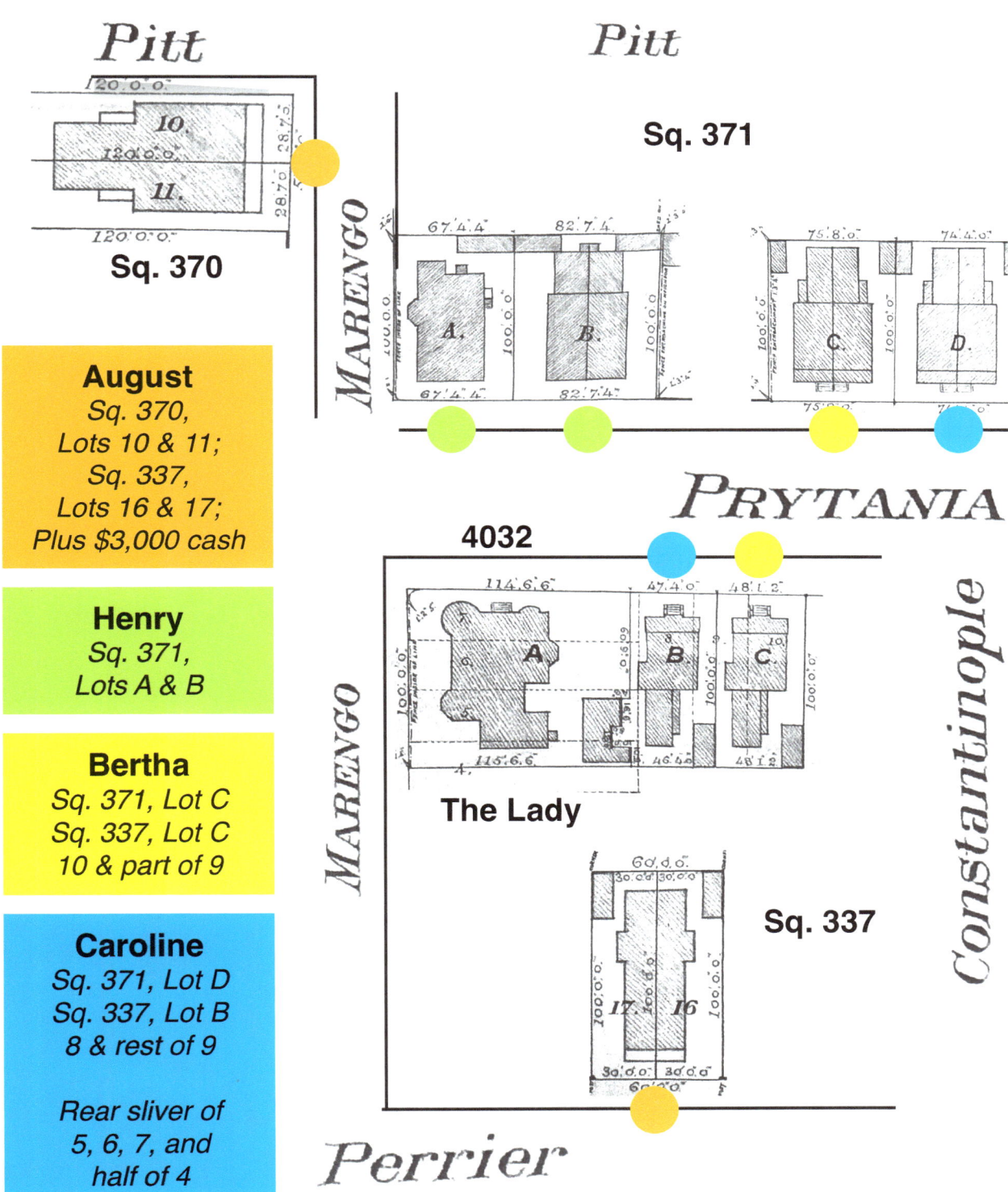

August
Sq. 370,
Lots 10 & 11;
Sq. 337,
Lots 16 & 17;
Plus $3,000 cash

Henry
Sq. 371,
Lots A & B

Bertha
Sq. 371, Lot C
Sq. 337, Lot C
10 & part of 9

Caroline
Sq. 371, Lot D
Sq. 337, Lot B
8 & rest of 9

Rear sliver of
5, 6, 7, and
half of 4

Chapter 2: History of Property

On April 2, 1911, The Lady was put up for sale.

On January 28, 1913, August H. and Henry H. Flaspoller sold The Lady to their sisters Bertha Anne Flaspoller, divorced wife of William Drott, and Miss Carrie Flaspoller for $6,000.00.

On June 30, 1918, 4032 Prytania was listed for sale for $12,000.00.

On February 16, 1919, the sisters sold The Lady to Jacob Klein and his brother Leopold for $9,250.00. The $9,250.00 was to be paid with a cash payment of $2312.50, with the remaining $6937.50 to be paid in three payments of $2312.50. These payments were to be made each year for three years.

The property had been advertised for sale in 1918 for $12,000.00. This price was probably used because the sisters had purchased their brothers' half share for $6,000.00. It sold in 1919 for $9,250.00 because with no electricity and very little plumbing, it would have been a hard sell.

Chapter 2: History of Property

After the sale, the contents of The Lady were auctioned. As you read, the contents give you an idea of what the interior looked like as a single family home.

> April 9, 1919—The auction of the Valuable Household effects of the Flaspoller Home, 4032 Prytania St.
>
> Harry Fitzpatrick, Auctioneer, 225 Royal St.
>
> Mahogany and leather Parlor Suite, 2 Crystal Chandeliers, Massive Mahogany Bookcase, Handsome overstuffed Parlor Pieces, Haywood & Wakefield Living Rooms Sets in Wicker, Handsome Antique Buhl *(German spelling of the word Boulle, pattern inlays of brass, tortoise shell, etc. chiefly French furniture from the 17th century)* Cabinet, Imposing Hall Rack and chairs, Floor and Table electroliers, very fine glass door, bedroom set, other bedroom furniture, Iron Beds, Bedding, Southern Belle Heater, Fine Oil Paintings, Water Coolers, Steel Engravings, many attractive Imported Ornaments, valuable carpets, Stair Strips and Art Rugs of many kinds, Mantel Cabinets, Mirrors, Richly overstuffed Box Couch, Bamboo Beds and Couches, Rugs, Mallings, Shades, Curtains, Drapes, China, Glassware, Chairs, Rockers, Tables, Safe, Utensils, Etc.

I wondered where the very fine glass door was located in the house.

The Klein brothers bought The Lady on February 10, 1919. At this time, the property measured 114.6 feet on Prytania by 100 feet on Marengo. On the bottom right of the map is a large two-story carriage house.

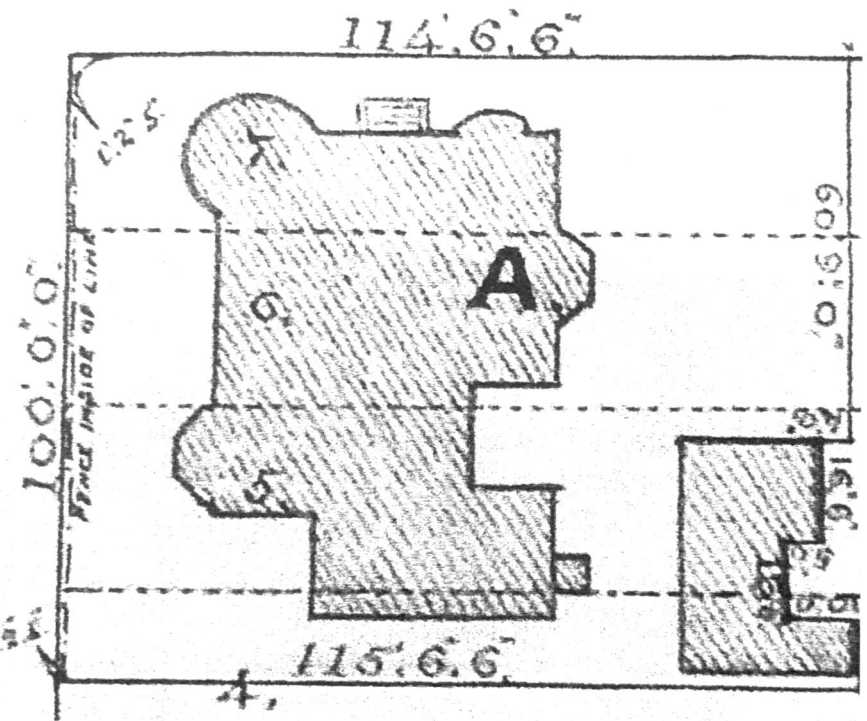

The Klein Brothers intended to convert the property into an apartment house. The building contract between Jacob and Leopold Klein and A. P. Boh & Co. was for "erection, alteration, repair, and additions to [4032 Prytania] ...as shown on drawings and as described in specifications prepared by Nathan Kohlman, Architect." The work was to be completed by September 15, 1919, for the sum of $9,000.00.

On July 1, 1919, the Klein brothers entered into a building contract with Kussman and Ellin Co., contractors. They were to provide plumbing and heating under the direction and drawings of the architect, Nathan Kohlman. The cost of materials and labor was to be $3,760.00. I could not find a copy of the work to be done.

The Kleins subdivided the property on December 24, 1919. The survey of the subdivision done on January 2, 1920 shows the property divided into Lots A and B. Lot A now measuring 79.6 feet front on Prytania contained the house. Lot B measuring 35 feet front on Prytania originally contained the carriage house. The carriage house is not shown on the survey map so I suppose it had been previously taken down.

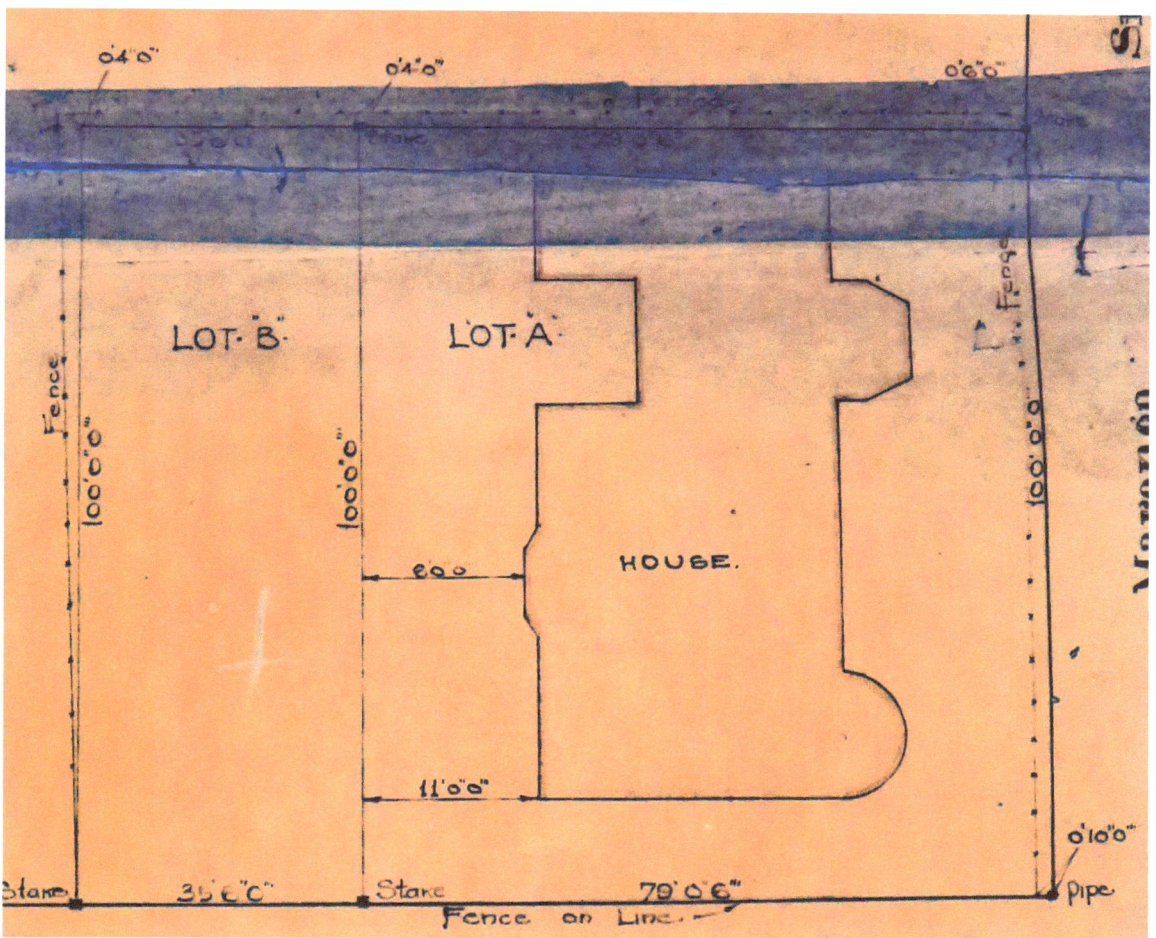

Jacob sold Lots A and B to Leopold on February 2, 1920. At the same time, he sold Leopold another property they owned jointly. Jacob died in 1922, so maybe poor health made him sell property at this time.

Leopold built 4026/28 on Lot B in 1921. On April 4, 1923, he took a mortgage on this property and improvements with Conservative Homestead for $14,000.00. The survey map done in 1923 showed the property to be 30 feet front on Prytania instead of 35 feet as on the subdivision survey in 1920.

The drawing below shows 4032 and 4026/28. At the bottom right of 4032 is a small bargeboard building where the carriage house used to be located.

I think the five feet removed from Lot B and added to Lot A was needed to build a small barge board building. This small building is at the back of the main house where the two-story carriage house was originally.

This additional five feet increased Lot A, including 4032, from 79.6 to 84.6 feet front on Prytania as it is now.

Ads to rent the ensuing Marengo apartments mention having janitorial services on the premises. Perhaps this was the purpose of the small outside building.

Leopold Klein sold the Marengo Apartments at 4032 Prytania to Victor Cefalu on January 4, 1924, for $43,500.00. The *Times Picayune* on May 6, 1926, reported the sale of the duplex at 4026/28 Prytania.

The Carriage House, which was two stories, is no longer. Mrs. West, the granddaughter of the Flaspollers, remembers it as being the nicest in the city.

In its place is a small barge board structure measuring approximately 12' x 30', which we call The Cottage. The picture shows repairs being made.

The Cottage is very close to The Lady and the house next door.

Maura Hudson's dog Ruby (above) and my dog Iggy (right), sunning on the ramp going to the back door of The Cottage. I built the ramp for my three-legged dog, Gita. All of the dogs are gone now. Still trying to combat grief with reason.

In the 1800s, individuals would use horses or carriages for transportation. Hitching posts were used to tie the horses, and mounting blocks were used to help mount a horse or enter a carriage.

In the backyard of The Lady is a large, flat stone. It was across from the back steps. I believe this was a mounting block. It is in a direct line to where The Carriage House was.

You can see the deliberate chip marks on all four sides of the block.

The house directly across Prytania has a curbside mounting block

I read that some blocks had people's names engraved on the side, and some were quite elaborate.

I wonder how many more can still be found in New Orleans.

CHAPTER 3

Outside Architecture and Gingerbread

The catalog pictured below, Roberts & Co., shows the years 1850 and 1891 and the words "New Orleans." Then, it states it is an "Illustrated Catalogue of Mouldings, Architectural, & Ornamental Woodwork." Following this is a list of woodwork items they have.

Most all of The Lady's exterior woodwork shown in this chapter can be found in this catalogue.

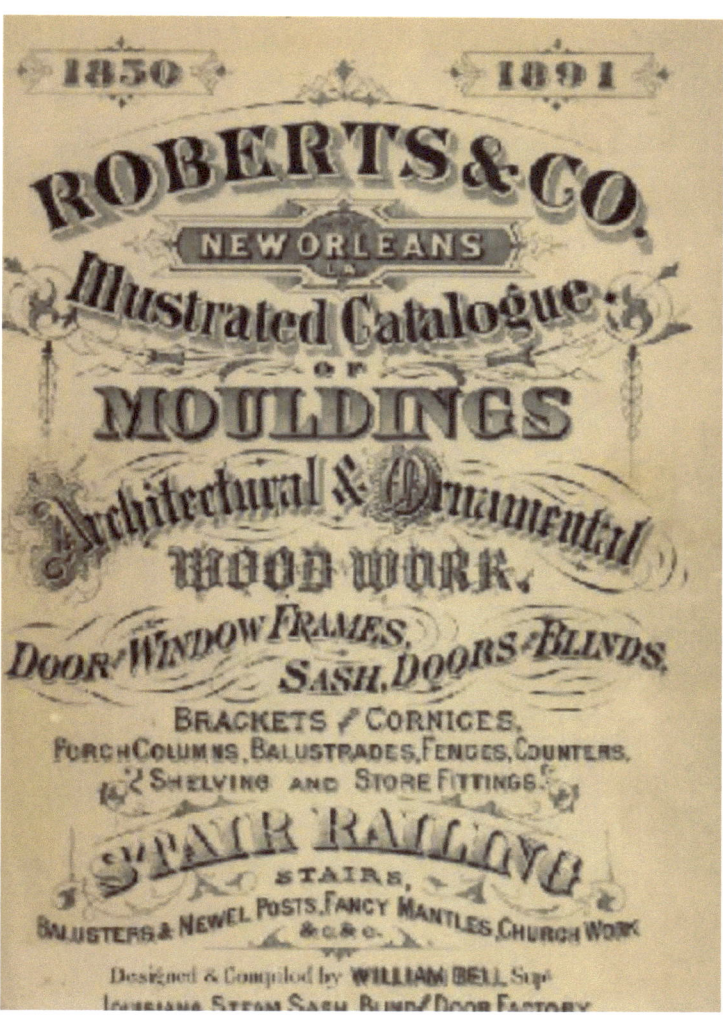

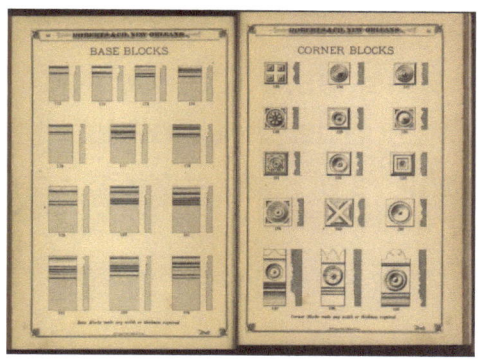

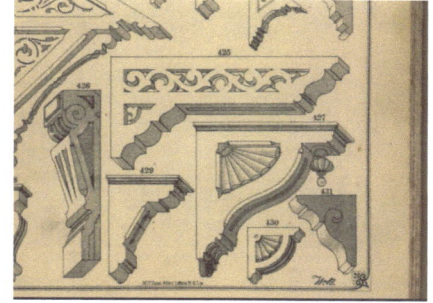

The Roberts & Co. catalog also had ads for other local businesses they recommended. For example, slate and terracotta for roofs, iron, both simple and decorative, concrete and pavers, and even watches and jewelry. You can find this catalog online as an archive.

Chapter 3: Outside Architecture and Gingerbread

Lee called The Lady's style of architecture Queen Anne. Queen Anne houses were not designed to have a sense of symmetry or balance. This house seems to exhibit signs of experimentation of this.

The house is on a corner and seems to be built to be viewed from the corner. The turret is located on a corner of the house and is surrounded by a large, ornate gallery.

A gallery is a long and narrow area. This gallery is the porch running on both sides of the house on the first and second floors. The ornate and unusual railings and top gingerbread attached to the gallery add a strong feature of symmetry to The Lady.

Photoshop-enhanced picture of The Lady by graphic designer Emily Eaton. This shows the railings and side entrance as originally built.

Gingerbread is a catch-all term to describe elements on a house used to make it more unique. These pierced and carved pieces of wood were formerly produced by hand. With the introduction of the scroll saw and steam powered tools, they were more available to everyone.

The Lady has many styles of gingerbread. The picture below shows a copper gutter attached to a board called fascia. On the fascia is a piece of molding called a cove molding.

Under the fascia board are a series of small blocks called dentils. These are embedded into a horizontal board called a cornice.

Whenever a piece of gingerbread was missing and needed to be reproduced, I would call Scott at New Orleans Millworks.

New Orleans Millworks, owned by Scott Taranto, specializes in historic architectural reproduction. Almost all the specialized moldings needed for repairs were made by them.

Dentils under turret on the third floor. The word dentil comes from the Latin dens, meaning tooth.

Dentils under porch

Dentils removed, repaired, and painted before replacing

Chapter 3: Outside Architecture and Gingerbread

The columns on the porch have brackets on both sides. Brackets can be both structural and decorative.

Porch bracket showing sunburst carved decoration.

All the brackets had been removed, repaired, and repainted.

Angelo La Martina, Neri Mencho, and Caesar Curuz put up scaffolding to do the last of the painting and replacing of the rebuilt and repaired gingerbread on the first and second floor porches.

Addition for bathroom added in 1909. Brackets decorated with sunburst pattern and end finial. The same style brackets were used in other places on The Lady. The sunburst pattern was the most used decorative element.

Chapter 3: Outside Architecture and Gingerbread

Shown here are corner trim pieces called quoins from the French word for corners. Quoins is pronounced "coins." They were originally made of stone and sometimes cement and used on the corners of stone houses for strength. These are made of wood but are used on corners to give an impression of strength. They can be seen on many houses in New Orleans.

Corbels and brackets both protrude from a wall. They support some structure or can be purely decorative. Corbels are usually thicker than brackets.

The pieces under the bay window would be called corbels. They are more decorative than for support.

The trim around doorways and windows is called casing. Blocks are elements used to make a neat way to end the casings. Blocks come in many different styles.

The block where the casings meet is called a bullseye rosette block. The trim above the block is called a crown.

This picture shows a bottom block called a plinth. This is used where the casing ends. Below the window sill is a decorative corbel.

This picture of a front gable with a bay window under it show many types of gingerbread. The top gable face has cedar shakes while the small gable under it shows a sunburst decoration.

The bay window roof has copper gutters attached to a fascia board with a cove molding. Under the fascia are dentils.

The top window and bay window have top, middle, and bottom blocks. Under the bay window's bottom ledge are decorative corbels.

There are two columns indented in the side of the bay window.

On the front wall edges are the quoins.

All horizontal wooden siding is called clapboard.

The siding on the front Prytania Street side and the right Marengo Street side is called drop leaf. This is a type of what is called novelty siding. These are the sides of The Lady that can be seen from the street.

Drop leaf siding

The siding on the side back porch was of the rustic log cabin style. It looked like logs used to build cabins but is really a thin board. This was the porch that was eliminated by enlarging and enclosing the space.

Log cabin style

The back and left side siding was the plain beveled type. These sides of the house could not be seen from the street.

Beveled siding

I have replaced most of the back and left side beveled siding with hardie board siding. This is made of cement reinforced with cellulose fibers. It is fire proof, water resistant, and has a 50-year lifespan. It comes primed and is then painted with a latex color of your choice.

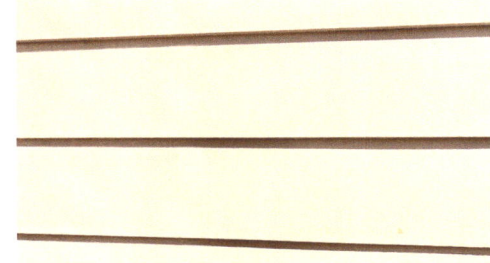

Hardie board siding

Mr. Rogers installed the hardie board. He and his installers were exceptional.

Chapter 3: Outside Architecture and Gingerbread

Dormers are prominent features of the roof of The Lady.

A dormer is a roofed structure that projects from a pitched roof. A dormer adds space to an attic and has a window which adds light.

There are different styles of dormers which are named by the type of roof they have. The Lady's dormers are gabled dormers because they have a gable-style roof.

Two popular roof styles are Hip and Gable. Both styles can have dormers.

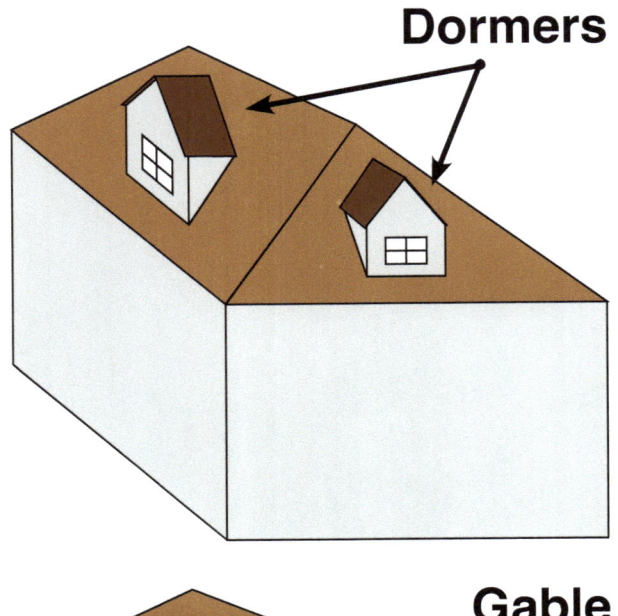

Dormers

On a hipped roof all sides slope to the house walls and meet at the roof ridge, which is the roof top.

The Lady has a hip roof.

Gable roofs have a pitched roof with two sloping sides that come together at the roof ridge. The roof sides are supported by a frame that rises vertically to form a triangle. This is the gable.

The gable roof ends enclose a triangular wall called a gable wall. Gable windows are in the gable wall.

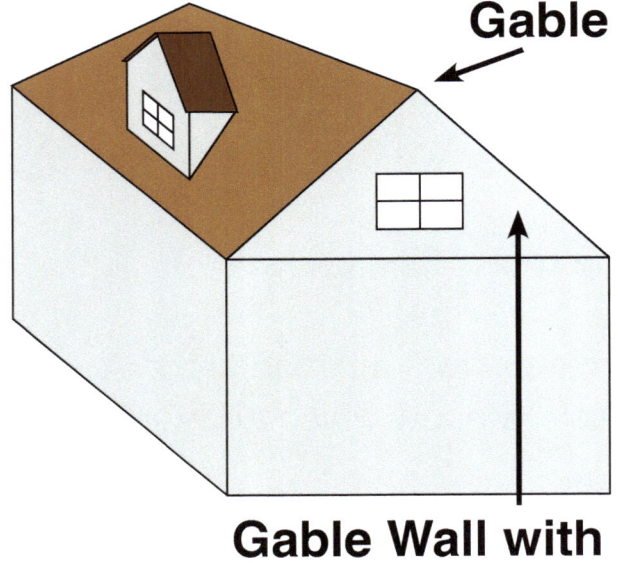

Gable

Gable Wall with Gable Window

A window in the end wall of a gable roof is called a gable window.

A window in a dormer is called a dormer window even if the dormer roof is a gable-style roof.

The pitch of a roof is the slope. An 8/12 pitch means the roof rises eight inches for every 12 inch increase toward the roof ridge.

A 4/12 pitched roof is not as steep as an 8/12 pitch roof.

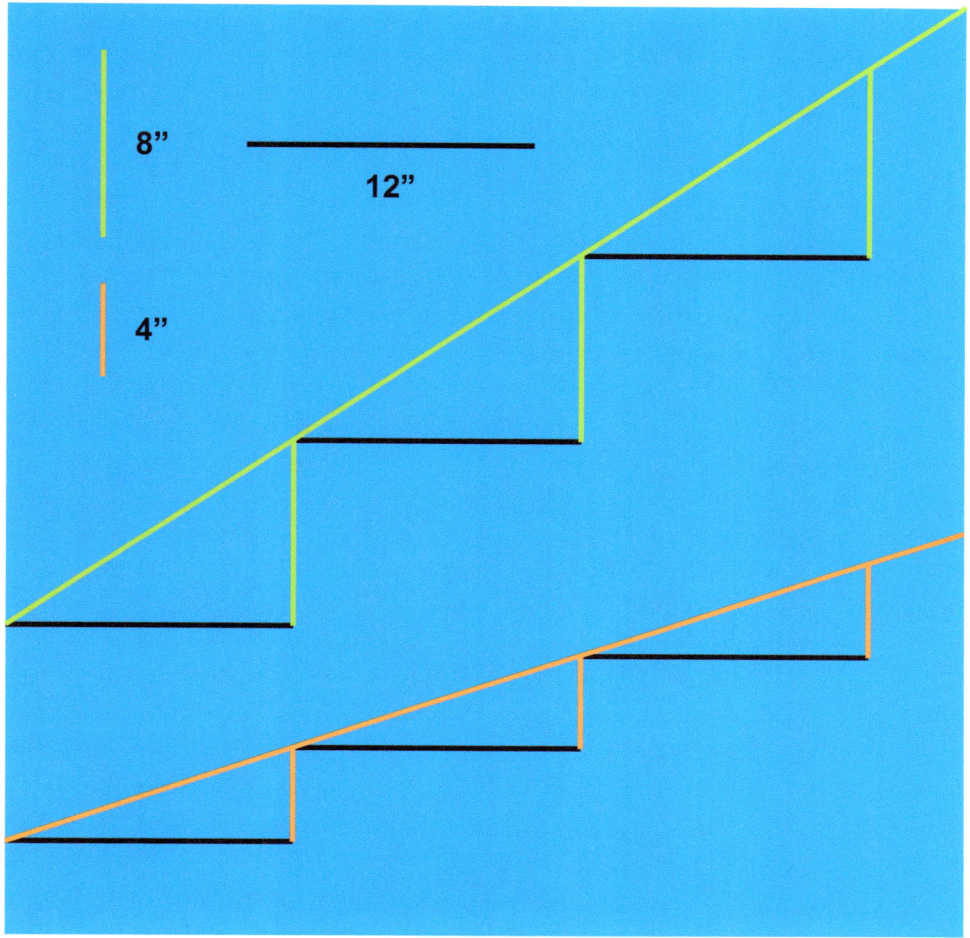

The Lady has a roof pitch of 12/12 which is very steep, but this pitch makes it easy to see the dormers and the beautiful pattered slate roof.

Prytania St. side showing dormers decorated with cedar shakes and the sunburst design.

The sunburst design was used on almost every decorative element, including brackets and dormers

Chapter 3: Outside Architecture and Gingerbread

These are the dormers on the Marengo St. side. The two small dormers have a window and the sunburst design.

Large dormer with window and sunburst pattern over bay window

Dormer support bracket with sunburst pattern and end finial

Chapter 3: Outside Architecture and Gingerbread

A bargeboard is a board which runs up the sloping edge of a roof. It is sometimes called a rake and is fastened to the projecting gable to give it strength. Bargeboards usually have decorative trim added to them.

A plain bargeboard would be called a fascia board. This gable does not have a decorative bargeboard. The decoration is on the dormer end and consists of columns and sunburst elements.

When you say "bargeboard" in New Orleans, you are referring to a type of house construction. Supplies were floated down the Mississippi to New Orleans on wooden barges. Once here, they were dismantled, and the bargeboards were used in many parts of house construction.

Example of a decorative bargeboard design

I thought the houses in New Orleans we call "bargeboard houses" were small, shotgun-style houses. I was surprised when I saw a bargeboard wall in The Lady. Below is a picture of this bargeboard I found when renovating an apartment. I now wonder if all houses built in the late 1800s were bargeboard.

In New Orleans, you might see a small house covered in cat claw vine and think the vine is all that is keeping the house from falling to the ground. These small houses are built of thick heart pine barge boards and so have considerable strength of structure.

Chapter 3: Outside Architecture and Gingerbread

The soffit is part of the attic structure. It is a ceiling used for roof overhangs. It can also be the underside of arches, balconies, and overhanging eaves. On porches, it forms the ceiling from the roof eaves to the siding. All soffits need to be vented to provide air circulation to the attic. On a porch, this ventilation can be seen as the round vents in the ceiling.

This lattice vent is in the overhang roof soffit of a small front porch. All soffit vents are air intakes into the attic. This air goes out the ridge or gable vents to keep the attic cool and dry. Notice the porch brackets' style are different than the ones on The Lady.

The gingerbread at the top of the porch would be called "pierced gingerbread." It bridges the gap between porch posts. Attached to the bottom of this gingerbread and the post are brackets decorated with the sunburst design.

The porch railings are quite different from the usual spindle type. Their more artistic design, in conjunction with the columns, brackets, and top pierced gingerbread, contribute to the defining face of The Lady.

Even though the railings no longer extend along the Marengo side, they are still quite imposing.

The turret has curved windows on all three floors. All of the windows on the turret have the same curvature. The window height becomes shorter with each increasing floor level, the first floor windows being the tallest.

The first floor front bay window also has a curved window, but the curvature is less.

After acquiring The Lady, I noticed the windows on the third floor turret were modern aluminum windows.

A tenant, John, told me there was a fire at the end of the turret caused by the owner using a small hibachi. John, at home across the hall, was able to help put out the fire. There was damage to the windows so they were replaced with aluminum ones. I later installed original style wood curved windows.

All the windows are operated using ropes and weights called counterweights. The movable parts of a window are called sashes. The combined weight of the counterweights must match the weight of the glazed window. When I removed the paint from a sash to show the beautiful cypress, the window no longer worked properly—it would slowly start going up on its own. The paint was probably lead-based and therefore heavy. I had to adjust it by removing some metal off the counterweights.

Curved window frame showing a groove for the rope for the window weight.

Window sash counter-weight

I found some old sinker cypress that was wide and deep enough to make the curved window sashes. Richard Stafford, a master carpenter, made a jig to cut the correct curvature. He used the jig and my bandsaw to make the window sashes.

Mr. Steve Rome, a wood turner and furniture maker, assembled the window sash.

Not only did I need glass for these sashes, but Hurricane Katrina damaged three others.

I replaced one in plastic called Lexon. It is like plexiglass but stronger. Then I found a company called Dependable Glass in Covington, La.

It is the most amazing place. They fabricate, bevel, or will work with you on a custom project if it involves glass. They have a showroom that is well worth the trip.

I brought the frames to them in Covington. I believe the glass was bent elsewhere, but they took care of getting the measurements and curvature correct and also mounted the glass in the sash frame.

Below is what two pieces cost me at that time.

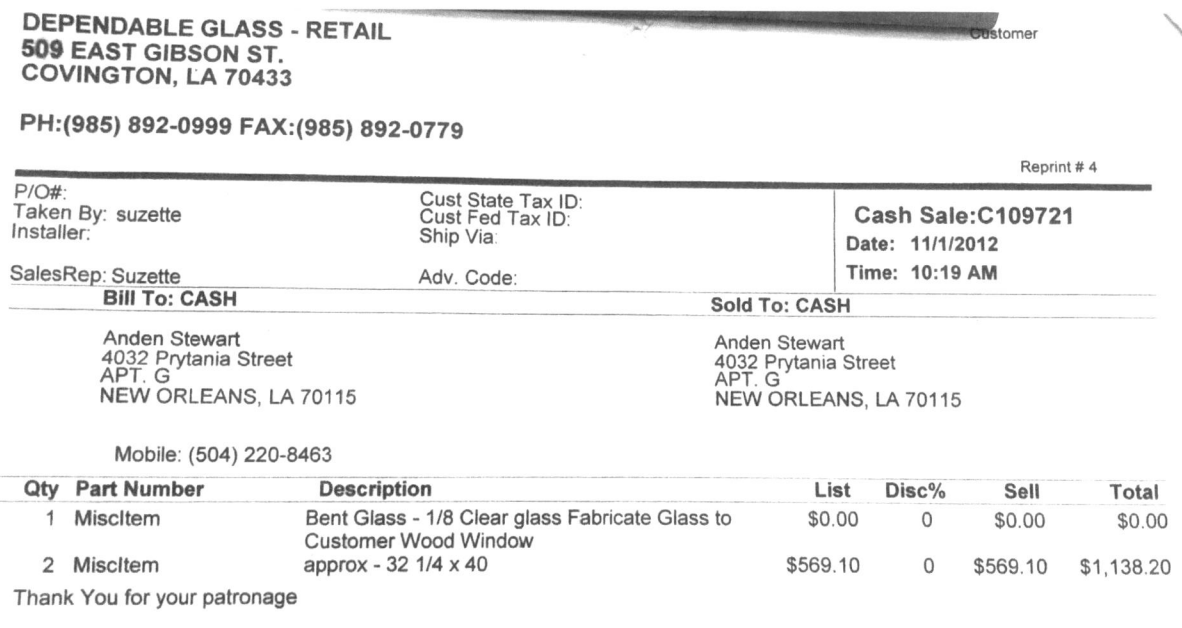

With tax, the cost for two pieces of curved glass mounted into my sashes was $1237.79.

There is a small foyer in front of the beveled glass door. The foyer is approximately 66 inches wide by 40 inches deep.

Top latch

Foyer floor latch hole

There is evidence that there was another pair of doors before you entered the foyer. On the floor is a hole for the bottom latch. The latch for the top of the doors is still there.

The foyer ceiling is made of cypress moldings with mahogany corbels going around the center. The black spot is a shadow caused by the spotlight used to be able to see the whole foyer ceiling. It had been painted white and hasn't yet been completely stripped.

CHAPTER 4

Changes After 1919 Sale

In 1919, she was savaged—cut up into 14 apartments. Fireplaces and mantles were removed, the porch railing on the Marengo side was removed, porches were enclosed, and a painted mural was covered. The side entrance was removed. There were access doors cut into the siding for deliveries to apartments on the first floor. A dumbwaiter was added where the side entrance once was to receive deliveries for the second floor apartments. The Prytania entrance now served as the main entrance for the 14 apartments.

Under the house where the side entrance had been, I found many pieces of decorative plaster. They must have come from very close to where the side entrance was. Throwing these plaster pieces under the house was probably a means of easy and quick disposal. I'm glad they did that, because it gives some other clues as to how the house once looked as a single-family dwelling.

These are the plaster pieces I found under the house where the side entrance had been. As there were fireplaces in nearly every room, they might have been part of mantles. Other possibilities are medallion ceiling moldings or decorative moldings on doorway passages.

Access to dumbwaiter inside the kitchens of Apartment F and G on second floor

In 1919, the side entrance was eliminated, and two dumbwaiters were put in to service the upstairs apartments

Some downstairs apartments had an access door cut into the outside of the house which allowed deliveries to that apartment

The dumbwaiter access doors served two apartments upstairs

The solarium was enclosed and part of the porch was taken to add a bathroom to an apartment. The porch railings that were on the side of the solarium were removed. The second floor railings were also removed.

Chapter 4: Changes After 1919 Sale

This picture shows how part of the first floor circular porch has been enclosed, and the porch railings on the first and second floor on the Marengo street side were removed. These changes destroy some of the look of the original symmetry of The Lady.

In this picture, you can see the original iron fence.

When I acquired The Lady, there was a chain link fence on the Marengo Street side. On the front Prytania Street side, there was a hedge made with ligustrum plants.

Sometime after The Lady was converted into apartments, mailboxes were added. The foyer side walls are beautiful cypress trimmed with mahogany.

Left side panel

Right side panel

The hole for the pushbutton is on the panel on the left side of the foyer

In one of the large panels is a hole that appears to be where a push buzzer was located. This was probably used to call someone in the house when it was apartments. Some of the ads to rent the apartments mention a janitor on call.

CHAPTER 5

Interior Changes After Sale in 1919

Chapter 5
Part 1:
1st Floor Interior

First Floor as Mrs. West Remembers It

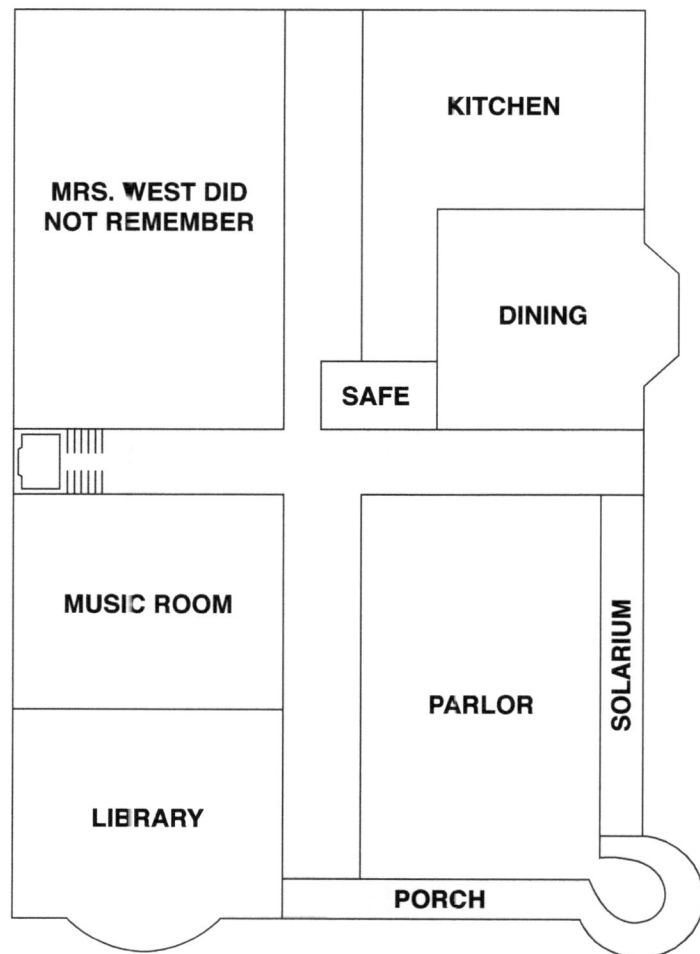

Below are a few of the more general things Mrs. Estelle Flaspoller West remembers about The Lady.

There was no electricity in the house. All light came from gas lamps. The only method of heating came from the fireplaces, there being a fireplace in most every room. It was basically a dark house decorated with shades of red and brown. There were chandeliers with lots of prisms on them. The house had beautiful wide-plank heart pine floors but had wall-to-wall carpeting covering them. There were two sets of carpeting: one that was rather thin and could later be thrown away—this was put down in the summer—and another set of darker carpets that were put down in the winter. There was also a very small set of steps at the back of the house between the walls that the servants used.

At this time the floors had no subfloors, so rugs would be necessary to keep out any drafts from between the floor boards.

Chapter 5.1: Interior Changes: 1st Floor

Back Half of First Floor

Mrs. West did not remember anything about this room.

Mrs. West did say the kitchen was very large and filled with the most up-to-date utensils and appliances.

The "safe," what we would call a pantry, was right off the dining room.

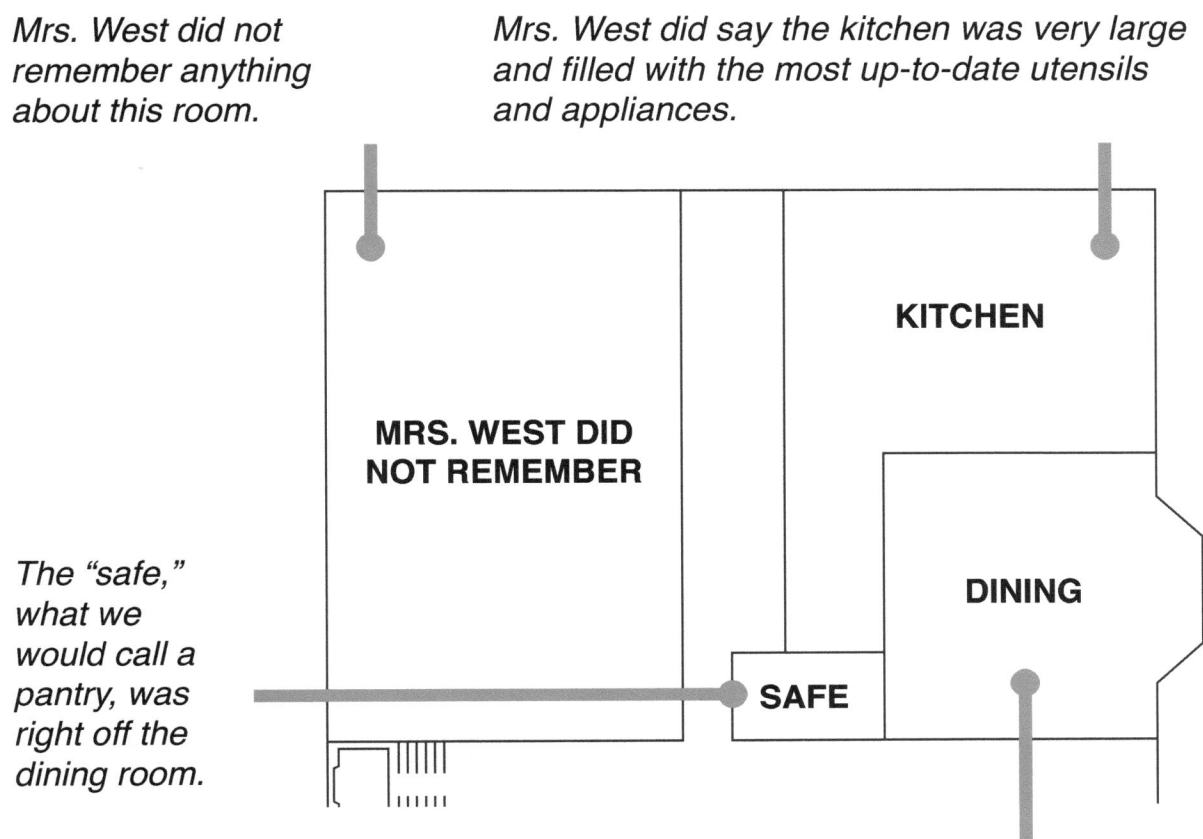

The dining room was very large with a table that could seat at least a dozen people. Close to the dining room was a large sideboard full of china and silver. There was a large window between the dining room and the kitchen through which the cook passed the food to the maid who served it.

The area Mrs. West did not remember was a small porch and a kitchen.

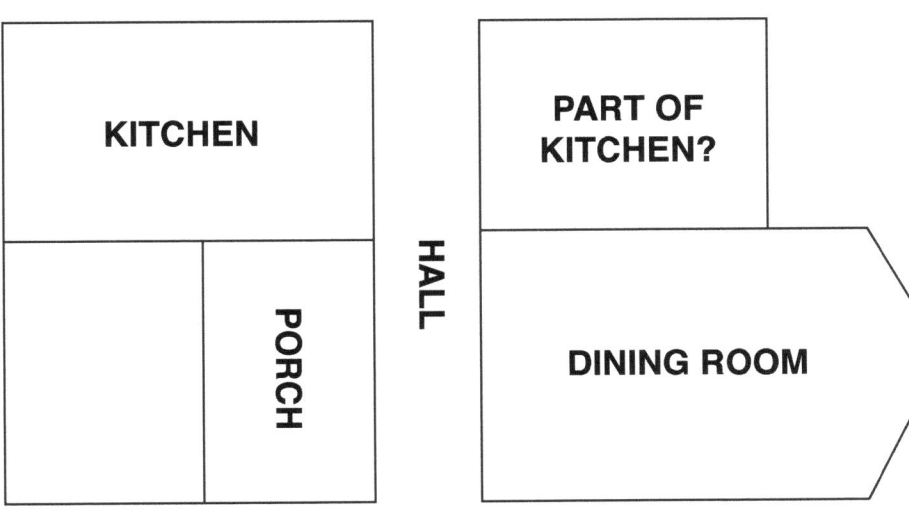

Front Half of First Floor

Mrs. West said that the music room was the most open, brightest, and happiest room in the house. It was in this room that the family actually lived and played.

All well-brought-up young women were expected to be able to entertain a party by playing the piano or some other musical instrument, or by singing.

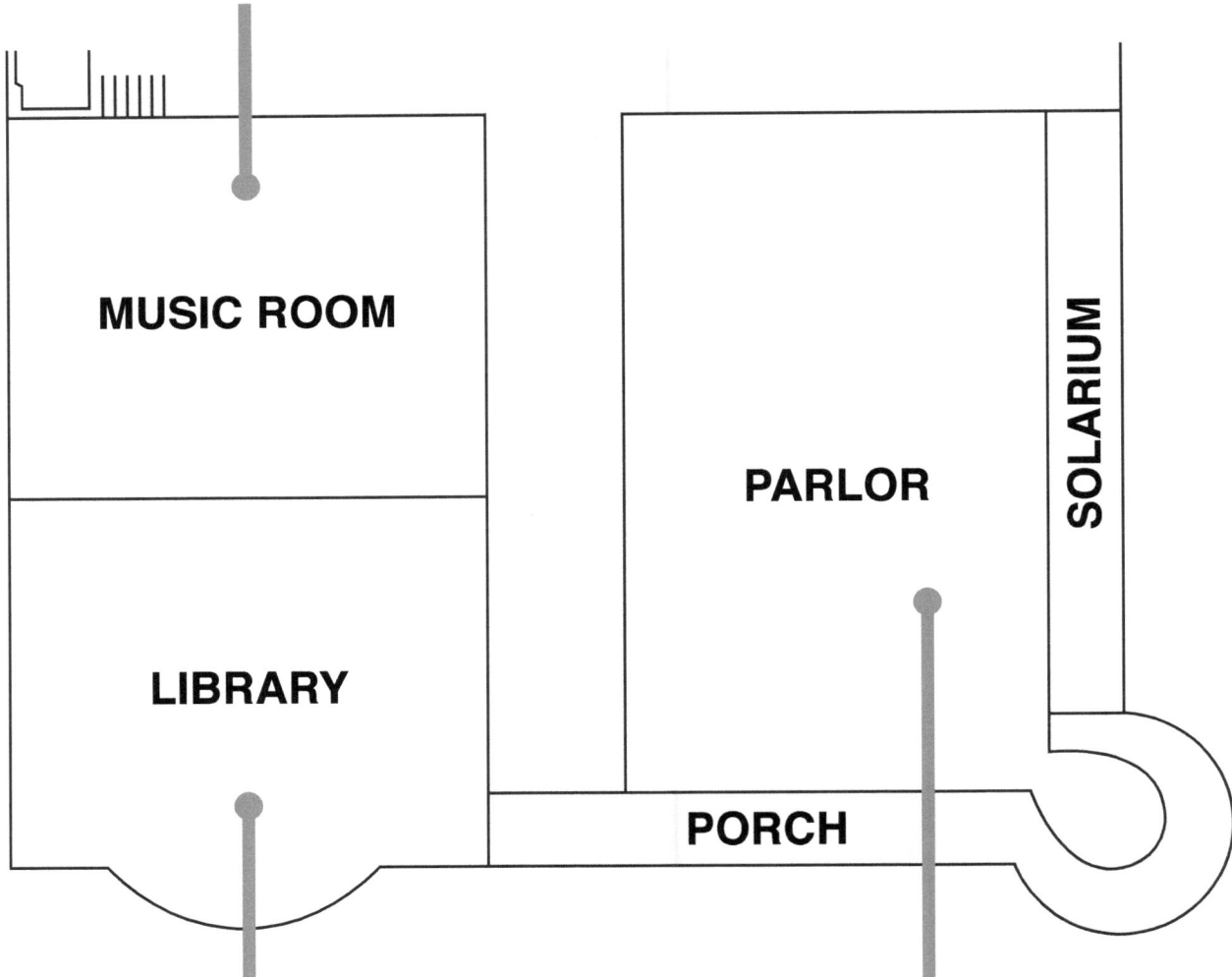

Mrs. West said the library was very dark with massive, ugly furniture, but Mr. West says he courted Mrs. West in this room. He remembers sitting in the alcove in the bay window.

The first room on the right, called the parlor, was only used for special occasions. It was very elegant. There was gold leaf on moldings, mirrors, and picture frames. Children were not allowed in this room.

This is a more accurate drawing showing a front entrance, side entrance, back porch, small back chimney, side porch, and cistern. Shown also is a serving window across from the dining room, a room called a safe, and a cypress sideboard. The serving window and the cypress sideboard are still there.

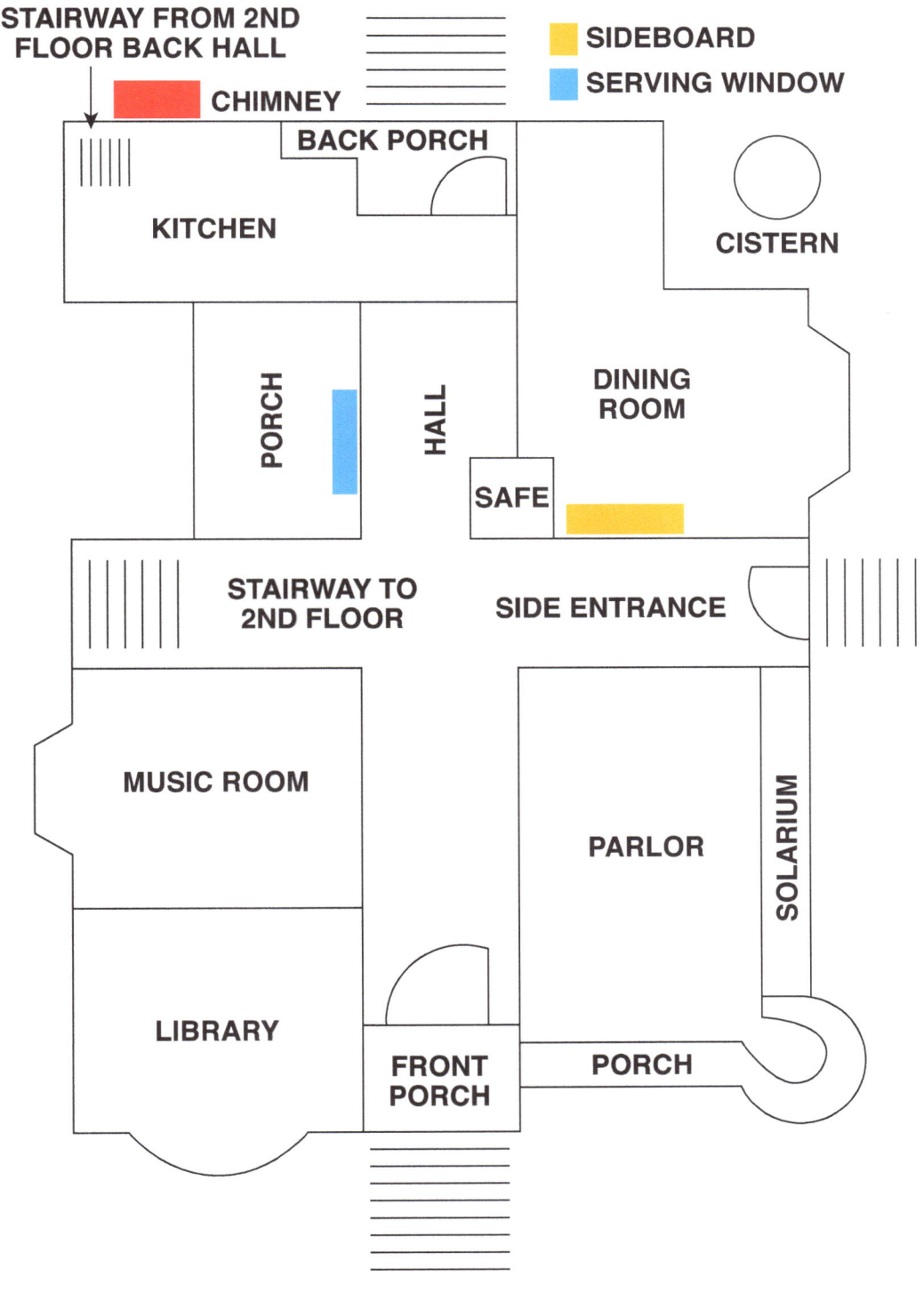

Mrs. West remembers a large sideboard which contained china, silver, glass, etc. A sideboard is a flat-topped piece of furniture with cupboards and drawers which would be placed along the wall and used for storing dishes, glass, and table linen. This one is quite beautiful and made of cypress and glass. It is part of what is now Apartment C.

Mrs. West also mentioned a large window between the kitchen and dining room. This was used to pass food from the kitchen to the ones serving the food. The serving window is still in the wall.

The First Floor as I Found It

The Lady was divided into 14 apartments, labeled A through N. On the first floor were six apartments: A, B, C, D, K, and M. I believe apartments K and M were added last. Apartment L was the outside cottage.

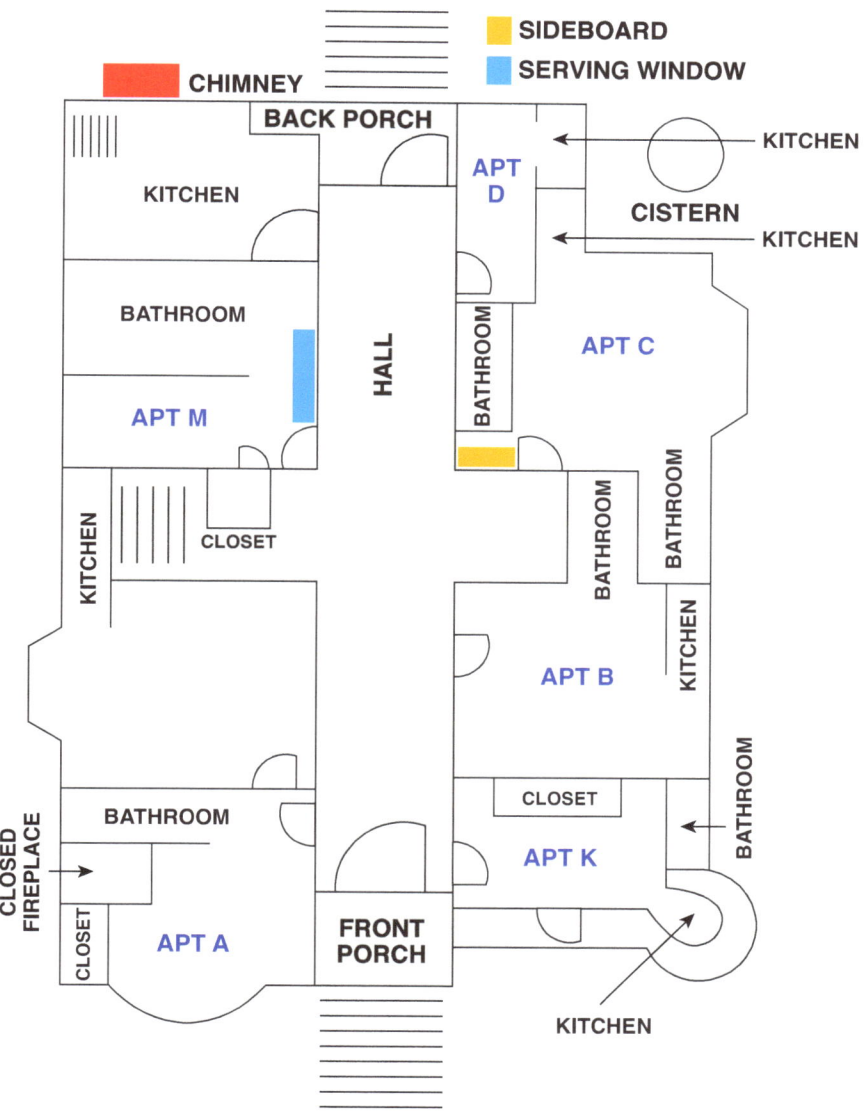

Major exterior changes when converted into apartments:

- Side entrance removed
- Solarium enclosed and outside railings removed
- Part of circular porch taken for bathroom
- Front entrance damaged with addition of mailboxes
- Side back porch enlarged and enclosed

This is the first floor now:

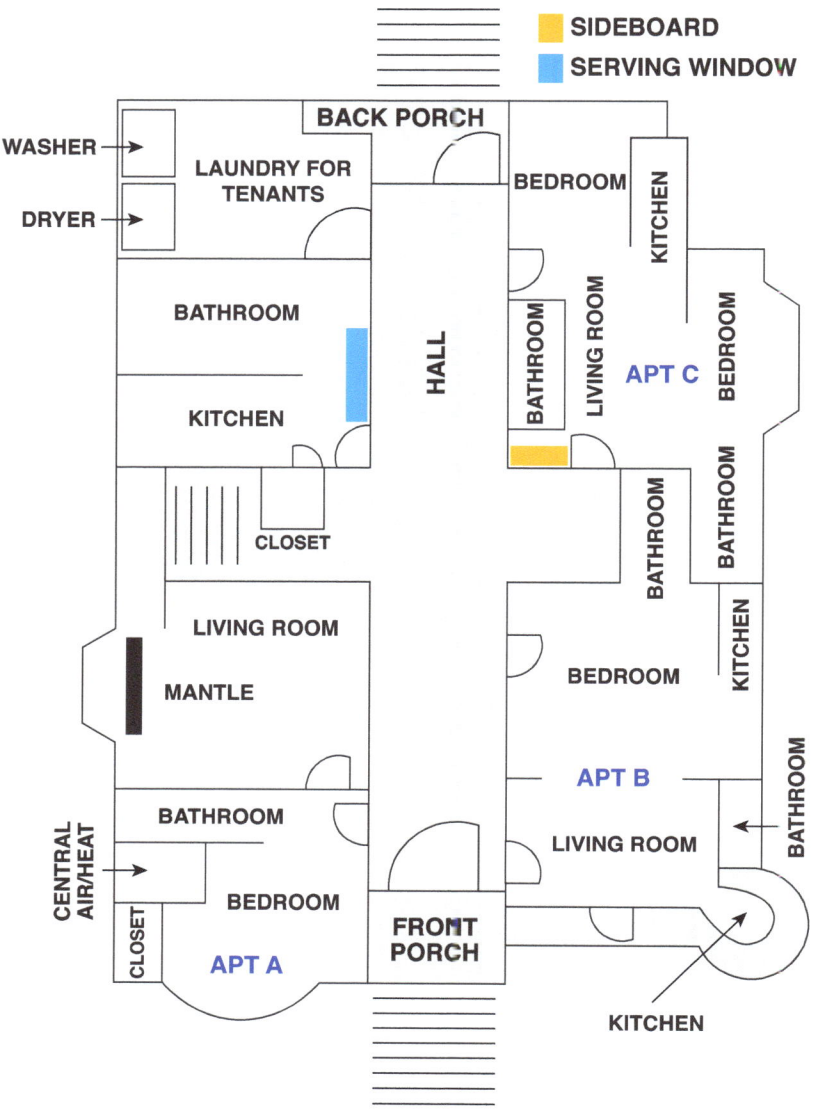

By combining some apartments, the number of apartments went from 14 to 10. Now there are nine in the house, the 10th being the outside cottage. I sheetrocked and renovated bathrooms and kitchens. Five apartments have central air and heat, while others have heat and cool units.

Renovating Apartment A

There was a small closet I wanted to enlarge. When I removed the small closet's back wall, I found this wall painting.

The painting started under an elaborate gold-colored plaster molding and ended at the top of the picture molding. I think it originally wrapped around the whole room.

Chapter 5.1: Interior Changes: 1st Floor

In 1919, the Kleins put in a gas line and signed a contract with Kussman and Ellin to put in plumbing and heating. The materials and labor were to cost $3760.00.

Mr. John Carboni, who works for Entergy, got a copy for me of the order to put in the gas line in 1919. The copy of the order below shows the gas line was ordered by L. Klein. It shows he paid $55.00 on September 3, 1919 for this to be done.

There is a small room on the back porch which we call the meter room. Originally, both electric and gas meters were in this room, but now there are only gas meters.

I believe the wainscot shown in the room is there because it was part of the original kitchen.

This must have been the original electric service box. I do not know when it was put in.

Chapter 5.1: Interior Changes: 1st Floor

At different times throughout the years, the gas meters were serviced or replaced. At these times, the men who did the work would write their name and date on the wall. The wall is not in good shape, but you can still see some of these writings. Mr. John Carboni signed the wall on March 28, 2001. He was the one who gave me the 1919 copies of the gas line run. He also provided me with some of the last names shown here.

The first writing visible said:

Gas meters re-checked by Margiotta 2/21/22.

Others read as follows:

Big John [Schmit] on job + Green 3/13/69

B & B was on job first HA HA

12/8/75 (in white chalk)

(Faint date) '92

Changed meters John [Carboni] & Tom 3/28/01

Scott [Martinez] was here 11/25/09

When I purchased The Lady, I found there was only one water meter. I was surprised to find that the hot water seemed endless but took some time to get to some apartments.

There was a large hot water heater. However, the reason the hot water seemed endless was that there was a large storage tank mounted above the hot water heater.

I had to remove the storage tank, as the bottom was rusted and leaking.

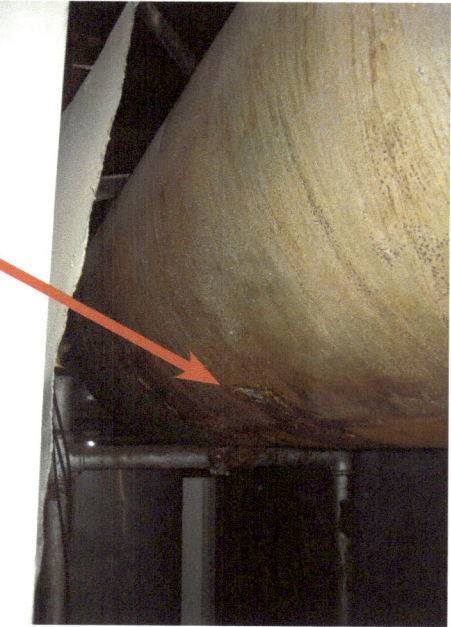

You can see how large the storage tank was by this picture.

Carl Davis ("Bones") could almost sit upright in it.

A Sawzall was used to cut up the tank.

This was the amount of scale inside the storage tank.

Looking under the house, my plumbers Melvin and Alvin Munch noticed a pipe that seemed to have been at one time connected to the hot water heater. Hot water would go to each apartment, then dead-ended at this disconnected pipe.

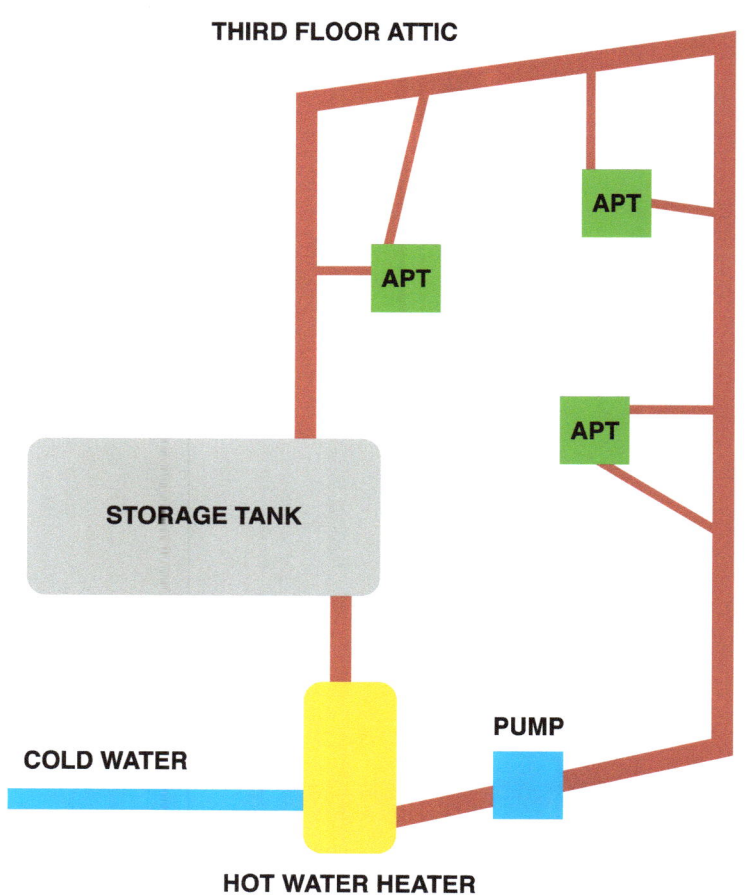

Once the pipe was reconnected to the hot water heater, hot water circulated to each apartment and then returned to the hot water heater. Hot water was available at each apartment almost instantly, no matter how far away it was from the hot water heater.

Hot water leaves the heater by rising to the storage tank, then to the third floor attic, and back to the hot water heater. Hot water goes to each apartment, which returns to the main line.

We added a pump to help circulate the hot water, but when the pump quit working we realized it wasn't necessary.

Thermodynamic system: hot water rises therefore circulates when connected in a closed system.

The rooms in The Lady were originally heated by fireplaces which burned coal. The fireplaces were closed and covered over, and the mantles were removed in 1919.

When I acquired The Lady in 1967, the rooms were heated by radiators similar to the one shown here.

In 1919, the Kleins put in a gas line and signed a contract with Kussman and Elklin to put in plumbing and heating. The materials and labor were to cost $3760.00.

This was probably when the radiators were put in.

I took them out, as they had scorched the floor and walls in some of the rooms. I replaced them with space heaters, then central systems and window units.

Chapter 5
Part 2:
2nd Floor Interior

Chapter 5.2: Interior Changes: 2nd Floor

Mrs. West describes the second floor as having four bedrooms, a plunder room, a sewing room, and a servants' room.

The plunder room was a catch-all room where things were stashed away.

Several times a year, a seamstress would come and sew for the family. She would use a room called the sewing room.

There was also a back stairway for the servants' use. This allowed the servants to access the first floor without using the main stairway.

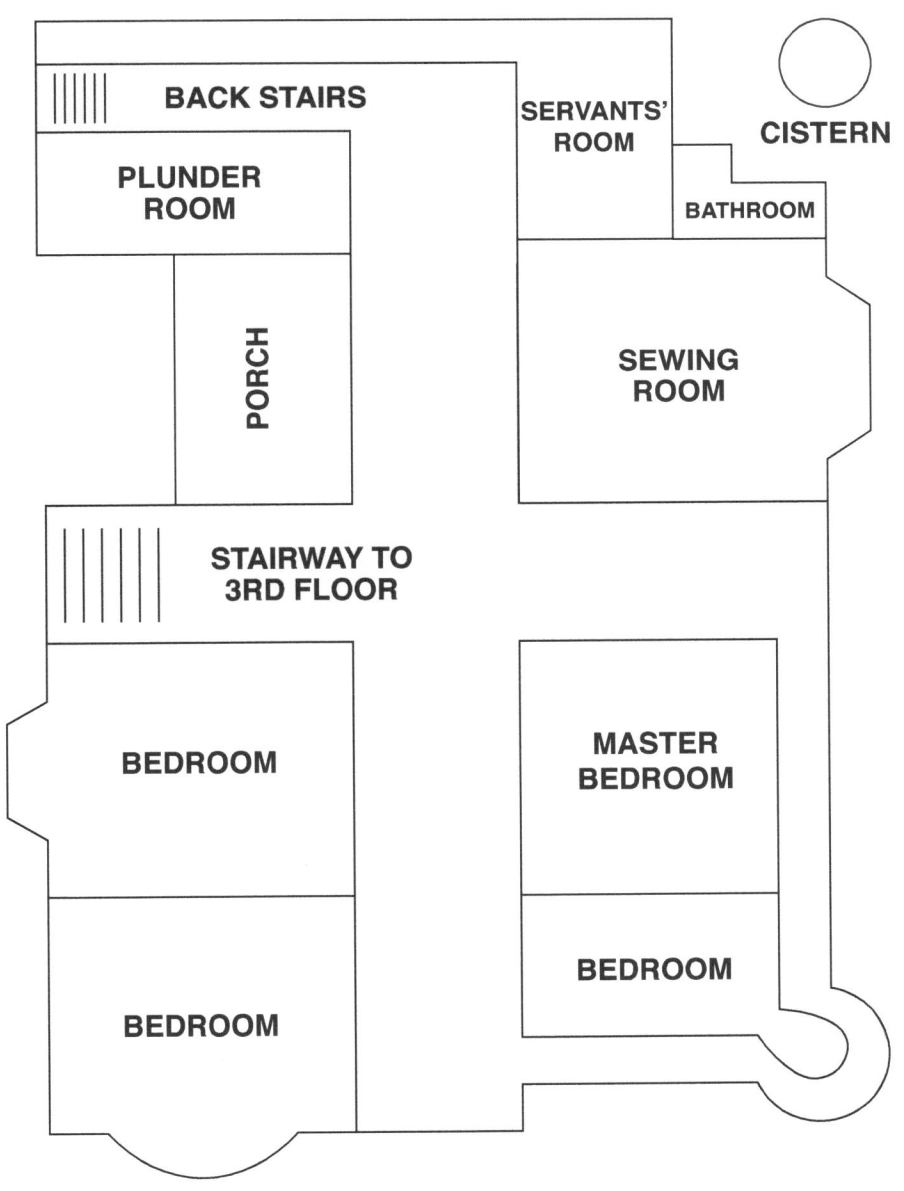

Chapter 5.2: Interior Changes: 2nd Floor

There were many changes when the second floor was cut up into five apartments. The major changes were enlarging and enclosing the side porch and closing off access to the porch from the halls by adding rooms in these spaces. Areas where these changes were made are highlighted in blue.

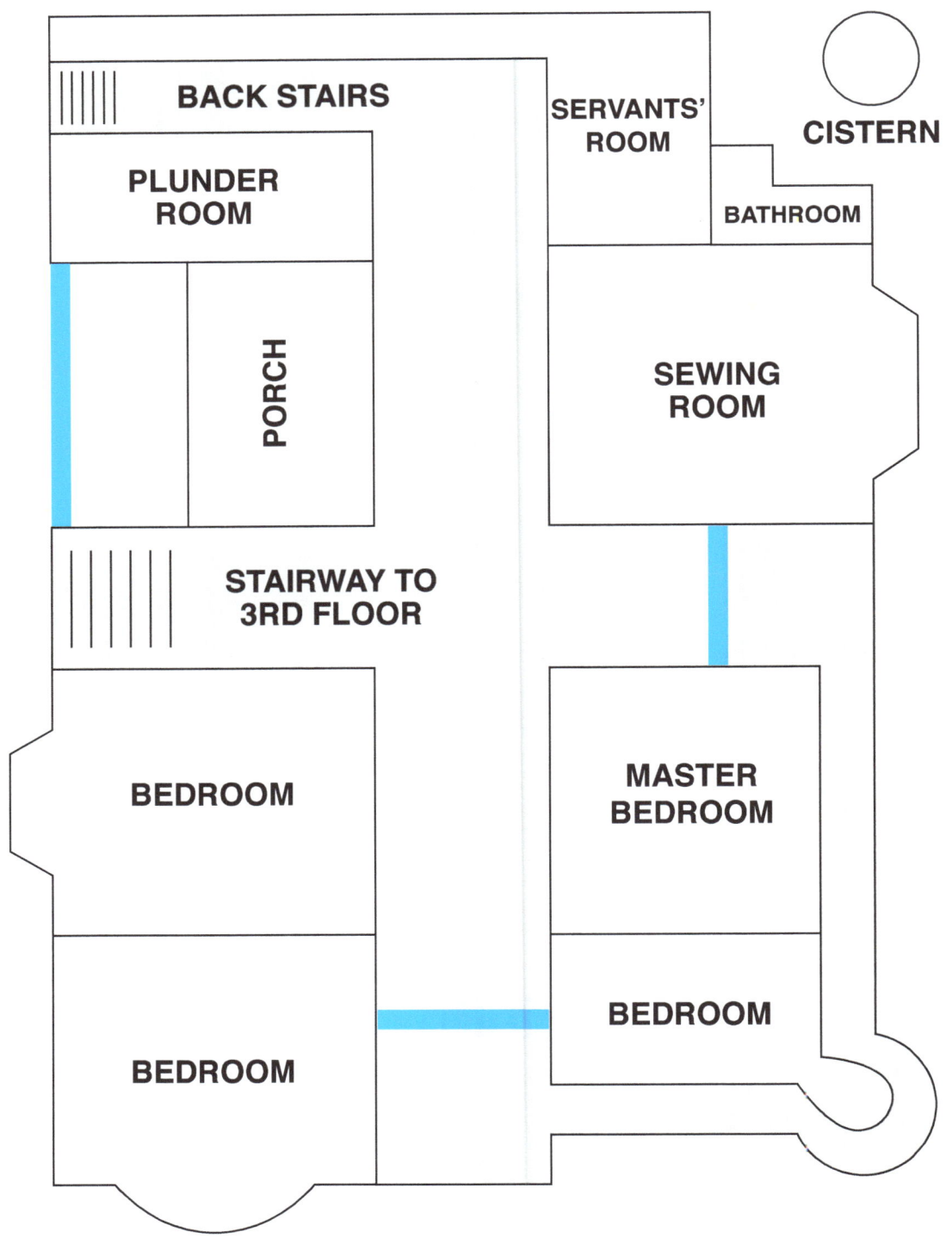

Chapter 5.2: Interior Changes: 2nd Floor

This is the second floor as I found it. It consisted of five apartments: E, F, G, H, and N. N was once the small porch which was enlarged and enclosed.

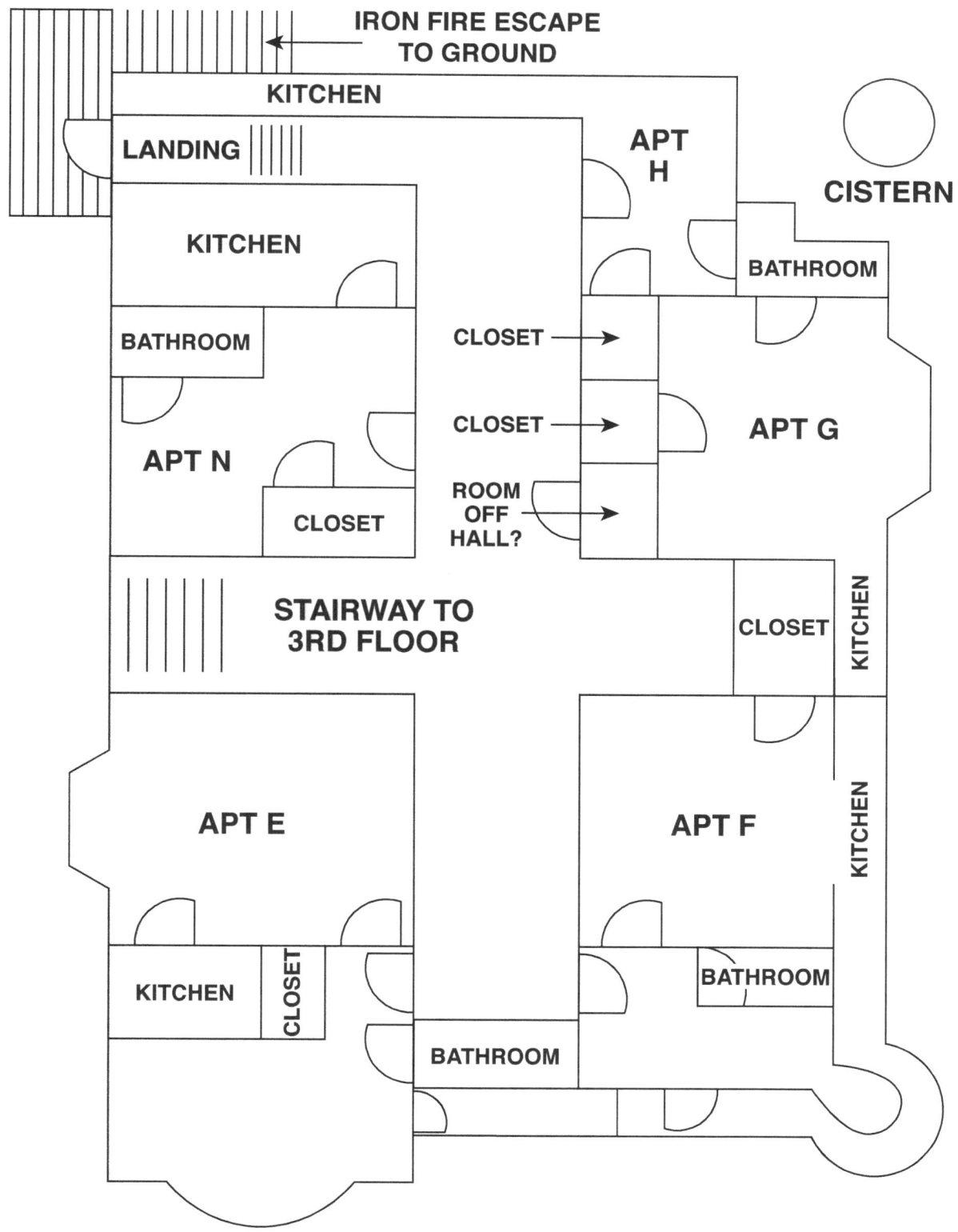

Chapter 5.2: Interior Changes: 2nd Floor

This is the second floor now:

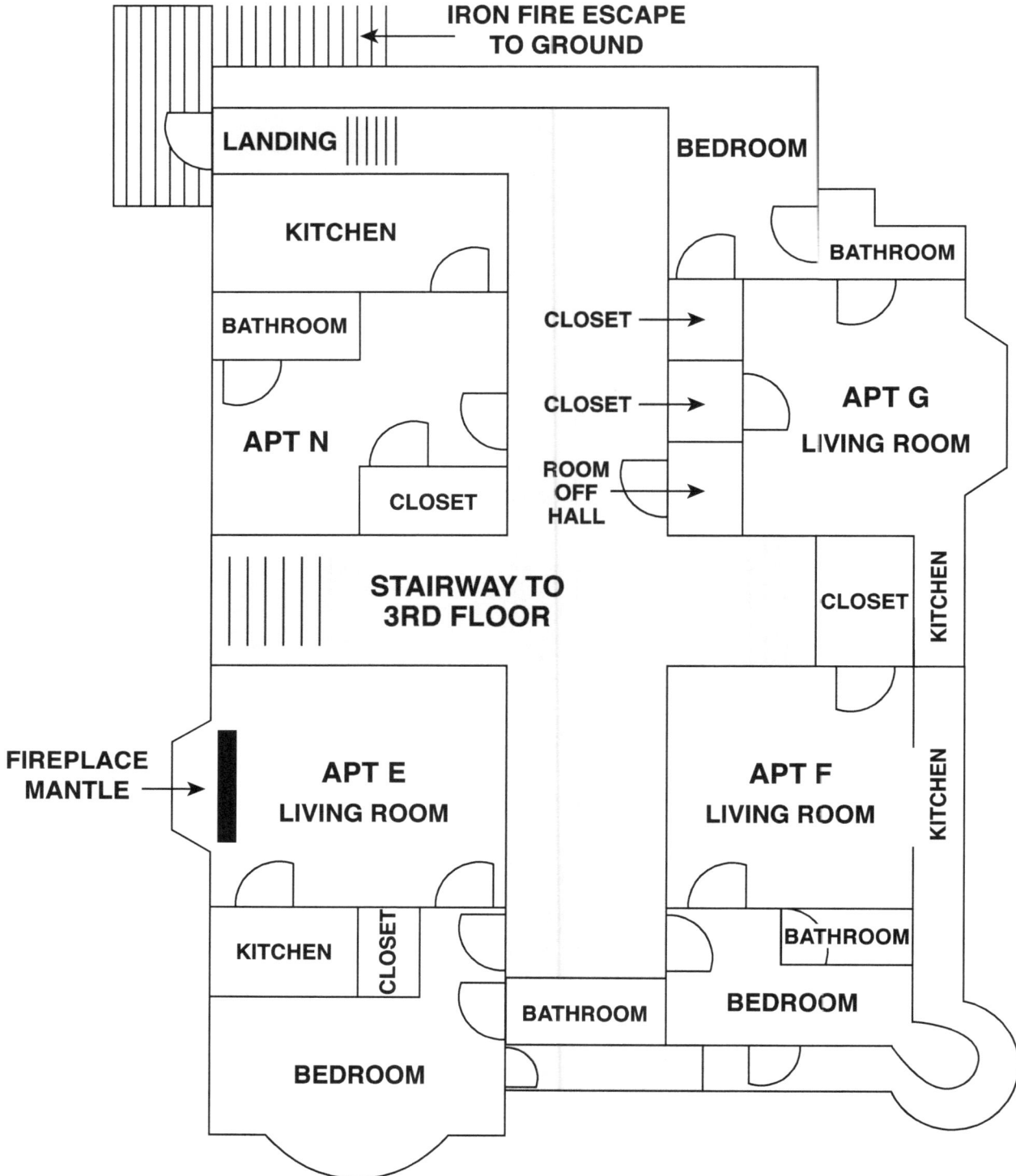

When renovating Apartment N, I found evidence of the original porch.

This is the wall inside Apartment N. It shows siding and an area which must have been a doorway to the open porch from the hall. The siding near the door is called rustic or log cabin style. It looks like logs, but is really a thin representation of a log.

In the corner by the door, you can see there were two levels of floor. The lower floor was where the porch ended. The higher floor was where the back room started.

This shows the window which is on the outside wall. This window would have been added when the porch area was enlarged. In the corner, you can see the siding and the outside board where wood called quoins once were. The quoins show this was the outside corner of the house.

The paint on the second and third floor hall walls was flaking badly. As we scraped the paint off the walls, the red color on the plaster was exposed. The interesting thing was that you could see the changes in the original hallway by the white plaster that was exposed.

These pictures show that the hall originally went through to the porch. The white area was where a wall was added, closing off access to the porch and making a room.

I thought the reddish-brown color you see here was the plaster primer. Mrs. West said the house was dark reds and browns. This might have been the real hall color.

Chapter 5.2: Interior Changes: 2nd Floor

The white plaster shows the original doorway opening.

I think this shows the hall was wider.

The cut in the baseboard shows it was added, which is more evidence the hallway was wider. This is also where a part of the hall was taken, closing access to the porch.

After removing the old paint I painted the halls a light cream color.

Stairways are called a "flight of stairs" because you use them to go up or down like an airplane flight. A landing is a platform where you step off a flight of stairs, or land. There can be landings between a long flight of stairs which give you a place to rest. There are also landings at the top or bottom of a flight of steps.

There is a center hall stairway which ends at a third floor landing. There are windowed landings between the first and second floor as well as between the second and third floor.

In another Roberts & Co. catalog, I found pictures of baluster railings and newel posts which were exactly like the ones found on The Lady's stairway.

The balustrade, which includes the handrail, balusters, and the newel post, had a black, rough surface. This is how shellacked wood looks as the shellac ages. I decided to remove the old shellac with denatured alcohol. I used a toothbrush, many paper towels, painters cloths, and determination to finally reveal the beautiful wood. I don't have a before picture, but here is an after photo. The balusters and railing are mahogany.

I found that three balusters were missing, so I called a friend and woodturner, Tom Dunne. He told me Steve Rome could do this for me.

Mr. Steve Rome, who also made beautiful furniture, made the balusters.

I later found out Steve Rome was the first president of the Bayou Woodturners. Tom Dunne, who recommended Mr. Rome, was the first treasurer. The club was started by Bob Sigilito in February 1999 with 19 members.

Fluted balusters and side step decorations are the same as in the Roberts & Co. catalog.

Newel post looks like the second from the right.

Newel post—mahogany inlaid with golden oak.

When I acquired The Lady, there was nothing on the top of the newel post. There were taped-off electric wires coming out of the top and an on/off switch under the stairs. Since Mrs. West said there was no electricity in the house, it would have been wired sometime after The Lady was sold. I don't know what kind of newel post light was used when the Flaspollers lived there. Perhaps it was one which burned oil.

Candles were used for light—they were even in chandeliers. Light was also provided by burning oil (fats like whale oil, etc.) and eventually by kerosene and then gas. The electric light bulb came with Thomas Edison's inventions.

I found and bought a typical newel post light from an antique shop on Magazine Street. These were popular in many New Orleans homes.

The lamps were originally made in England and France and were known as "Femme-Fleur." The lamp was usually of a woman accented with reeds and flowers. It was made of a white metal called pot metal or "spelter." This was covered with a brass- or bronze-like finish. Last, a lacquer was applied.

Examples of Newel post lights, shown in Roberts & Co. catalog of 1891.

Early newel post lights burned oil, then gas, and eventually were electrified.

The name on the plaque on the light is L'amour Galant. I intend to mount it on the newel post.

There are stained glass windows at each landing and also in the dormers on the third floor. Shown here are the landings between the first and second floors and between the second and third floors.

If the height between two floors is more than 12 feet, you have to have a landing.

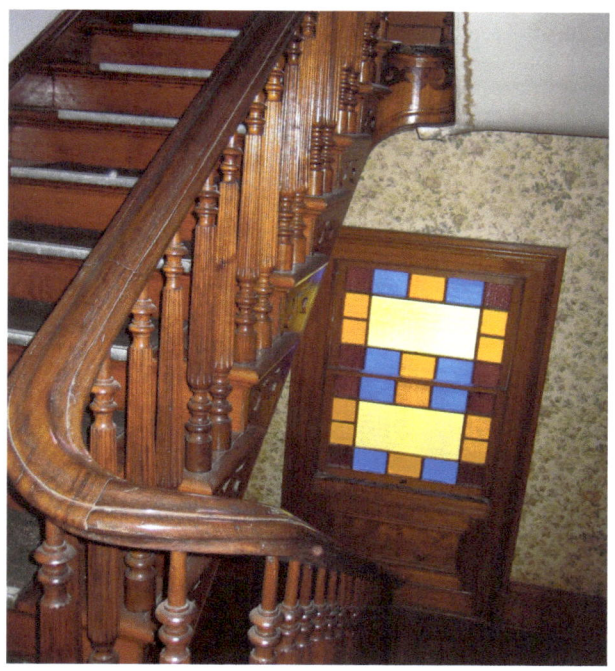

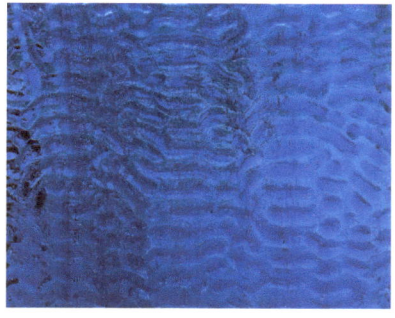
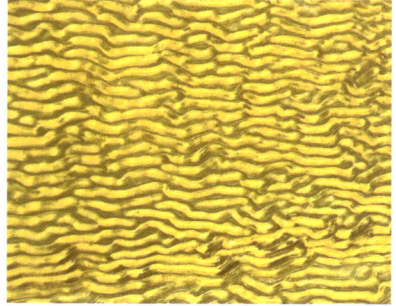
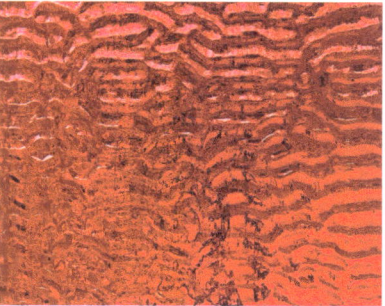

The pattern of the glass is called ripple glass. The glass colors are the primary colors: blue, amber, and shades of pink. By moving a window up or down, one color would be added to the other color, causing different colors to be formed.

Chapter 5.2: Interior Changes: 2nd Floor

The windows on the stairway are rectangular. The different windows did not always have the same shade of pink, blue, and amber.

The windows in the dormers have a curved top window.

Some of the windows needed to be repaired or rebuilt.

Chapter 5
Part 3:
3rd Floor Interior

Third Floor as It was Originally

Mrs. West continues: On the third floor was another servants' room and a large storage area known as the carnival room.

There were many trunks which contained Mardi Gras costumes. This was one of the children's favorite rooms.

On the third floor landing was the only telephone in the house.

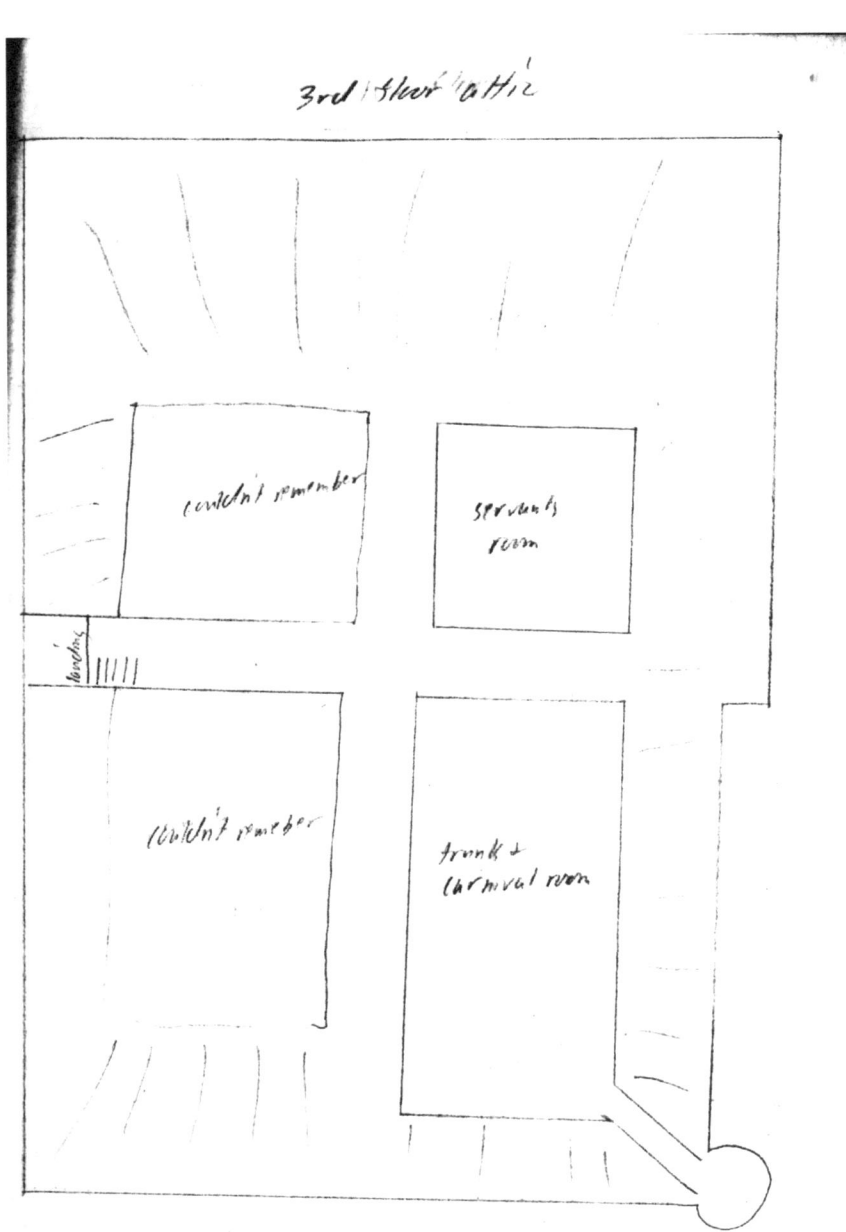

Chapter 5.3: Interior Changes: 3rd Floor

After the sale in 1919, the third floor was converted into apartments. This is how the apartments look now.

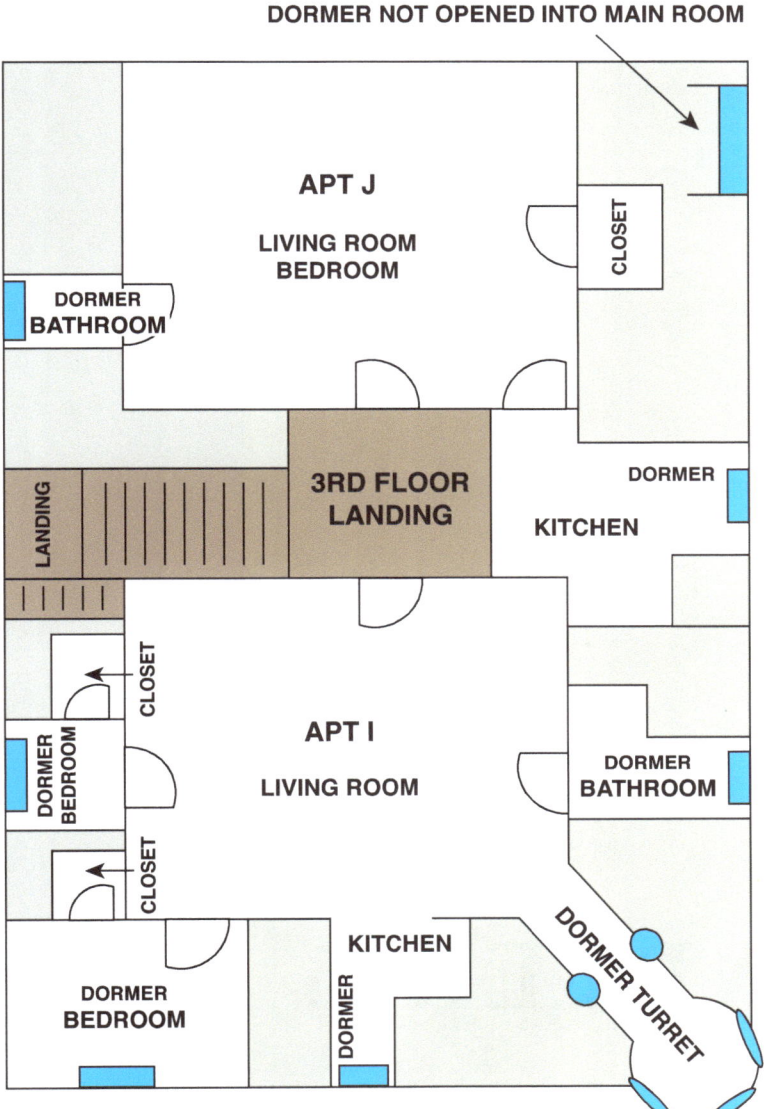

The stairway ended in a landing which branched off into two large rooms with dormers. These became Apts. I and J.

The dormers added architectural style and, as each dormer had a window, they provided light.

Location of dormer windows are colored blue.

Both apartments have been renovated. Apt. I has central air and heat.

CHAPTER 6

Damage by Time to Exterior

Chapter 6
Part 1:
Turret Repair

Chapter 6.1: Damage to Exterior: Turret Repair

Some damage by time was unavoidable. The turret and the gutters were made of galvanized metal, which has a limited life span.

There is a fancy cap on the top of the turret, which was badly deteriorated. We removed it and later replaced it in copper. The silver metal at the top was put on to keep the rain out of the attic until this copper top could be completed.

Years ago, I tried to protect the turret by painting it. One of my first carpenters went into the third floor attic from which he could access the inside of the turret. There was a ladder built inside the turret to allow you to climb to the top. Using the ladder, he attached a rope which he put outside the turret. Using this rope and what he called a Captain's chair, he swung around the outside of the turret and painted it. He was fearless. Phil Howard was his name. Unfortunately, I have no pictures of this.

 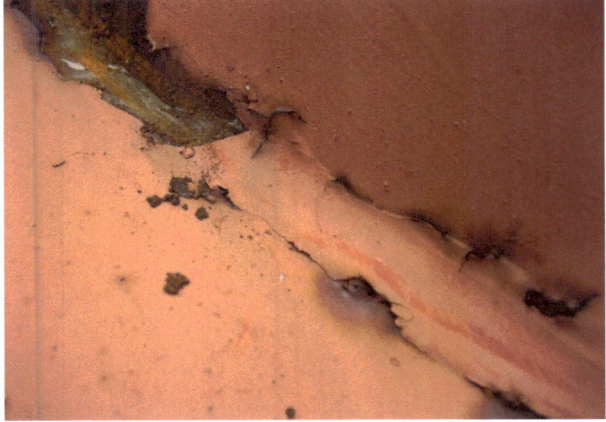

These are examples of the metal deterioration. Eventually, time had its way and the damage was unrepairable.

Chapter 6.1: Damage to Exterior: Turret Repair

After the storm Katrina in 2005, there were a lot of out-of-town roofing companies in New Orleans. I saw some copper roof work done by a company called Renaissance. I entered into a contract with them to do the repairs and replace the galvanized metal with copper for a total cost of $13,926.00 (the full invoice is listed in Chapter 9.5).

Scaffold built to remove old galvanized metal

When the old galvanized metal was removed, it was necessary to do some repairs

By going into the attic over the third floor, you could access the inside of the turret. You can see a kind of wooden ladder in the middle to enable you to climb to the top.

The black sheeting you see here is called Grace Ice and Water Shield. This is a rubberized asphalt formulation, which enables a watertight bond with the roof deck and acts as a barrier for both water and ice.

When you nail into the Ice and Water underlayment, it seals around the nail, as opposed to felt tar paper which does not.

The pink rosin paper is put on over black Ice and Water sheeting. The rosin paper allows the copper panels to move freely as they contract and expand.

Standing seam roof

Lock seam roof

Every roofer in New Orleans wanted to replace the turret with a standing seam roof. I wanted the original design called lock seam roof.

Chapter 6.1: Damage to Exterior: Turret Repair

Pictures of stages of copper replacement

Chapter 6.1: Damage to Exterior: Turret Repair

Picture of old galvanized metal turret top with fins missing

Turret top reproduced in copper

Turret completed with copper decorative top and with lightning rod. The solid copper rod was attached to the top and run down the sides of the turret by the Renaissance metal workmen.

The lightning protection system was put in by Mr. Bob Morris of Lightning Elimination Systems for a cost of $1500.00. He connected the lightning rod on the turret with all the copper gutters and downspouts.

He also advised me to put a surge protector in front of the electrical system. He said without this, if lightning hits the ground nearby it can go to the electrical system and destroy all electronic devices and appliances in the house.

Chapter 6.1: Damage to Exterior: Turret Repair

All of the gutters and downspouts are connected to the lightning rod on the turret top and then to the ground.

The original galvanized turret had a lightning rod attached to the top. It ran across the top of the roof and was grounded in the back of the house. It was made of a thick copper wire. At this time, the gutters were still galvanized metal.

Chapter 6 Part 2:
Roof

From a distance the roof looked fine, but as you can see from the pictures below, that was not the case.

Picture with my cat named Ivan the Terrible looking at a slipped slate in the gutter

The roof was slate and over 100 years old. I was constantly fighting leaks. I tried for quite a few years to maintain the roof. When a slate would slip causing a leak, I would call my roofer, Mr. Rudolph Schaff.

Chapter 6.2: Damage to Exterior: Roof

If the leak was on the Marengo or Prytania street side, he could use the flat metal roof, which was above the two porches, to easily get on the roof. He would then do the following: he would tie a rope to one of the foundation piers and bring the rope onto the roof. It would go over the top of the roof and hang down the other side where the slate was missing. He would attach a chicken ladder to the top of the roof ridge. This chicken ladder was a ladder which lay flat on roof and would be used to get to the area you needed to repair. My job was to get on the roof as high as I could and hand him the slate.

One day, I managed to crawl up a valley, which is where two roofs meet, and sit on the top of the roof ridge. King of the Mountain!

Valleys shed water from both roofs. There are two types of valleys—open and closed. An open roof valley is where the roofing material ends before the centerline of the valley and metal is used to bridge that gap. In a closed roof valley, the roofing material of both roofs meet. An extra layer of roofing material is placed over where the two roofs meet, giving a more finished look to the roof. The Lady has open roof valleys made of copper sheeting.

This is another way I tried to stop the leaks: I would go into the attic, and where I could see light, I knew a slate had slipped. I would slide a piece of thick plastic sheet above where the slate was missing. Then, I would slide the plastic down until the crack of light was diminished. I would then nail the end of the plastic still in the attic to the wood of the roof. If you looked closely from the ground, you could see pieces of the plastic flapping in the breeze. This worked well, and I wish I had some pictures.

I knew I really needed to replace the roof. In 2003, I was finally able to do just that.

The roof slate consisted of three different colors of slate laid in the pattern shown below.

I purchased the slate from Evergreen Slate Co. in Vermont in 1999 but could not afford to replace the old roof until 2003. The cost of slate, including bringing it to New Orleans, was $23,950.00 (the full invoice is listed in Chapter 9.5).

The slate colors are called Unfading Red, Unfading Green, and Vermont Black. The slate size is 10" x 14". This size is smaller than most slate used today.

The red slates were in surprisingly good shape even after 100-plus years. They still rang when you thumped them. The black slates were badly deteriorated, and the green were only in a fair condition. The different color slates all have different chemical compositions.

To calculate the amount of each color of slate to order was a challenge. This was because of the many gables and roof levels. I took pictures of all the different areas that were slated and counted the number of each color used.

I drew the pattern for the roofers to follow. Since I had pictures of all parts of the roof, I also told them what color to start with at each part of the roof.

There were four roofers. They worked in two groups of two. One handed a slate color to the roofer nailing the slate onto the roof.

Each roofer had a copy of the pattern.

Explanation of the Slate Roof Pattern

It is a simple repeating pattern, but I heard there was some cussing going on when a roofer would hand the installing roofer the wrong color.

Row 1: 1 Black, 1 Green, 1 Black, 1 Green (repeating)
Row 2: 2 Black, 2 Green, 2 Black, 2 Green (repeating)
Row 3: 1 Black, 1 Green, 1 Red, 1 Green, 1 Black, 1 Green, 1 Red, 1 Green, 1 Black
Repeat Row 2: 2 Black, 2 Green, 2 Black, 2 Green
Repeat Row 1: 1 Black, 1 Green, 1 Black, 1 Green

Each row is started mid-slate of the row below it.

The old roof slate had to be removed and repairs made to the old wooden support roof.

The wood roof supporting the slate was called open plank construction. There were small spaces between the boards which allowed the attic to vent and the slate to dry when wet from rain.

I chose to sheet over the original wood with plywood, then use 30 lb. felt over the plywood. I did this because with open plank construction, if you had a slate slip or become damaged, you would get leaks inside the house. The roof with a solid plywood backing would protect from leaks into the house. This time, all copper nails would be used to install the slate. The original nails would rust out, causing slates to slip.

There was a flat roof on part of the front of the house and on the Marengo side. I only had to scaffold the front and one side. The scaffolding was from United Scaffolding in LaPlace. The total cost to scaffold was $6451.68 (the full invoice is listed in Chapter 9.5). This cost included setup, take down, and rental from April 12 to July 20, 2003.

Slate being brought to the roofers

Some of the roof caps were missing, but I managed to find some of them at the salvage yards in New Orleans. Others that I still needed came from Baton Rouge and Texas (these invoices are listed in Chapter 9.5).

Picture showing one chimney top missing and two of six copper vents fabricated as they originally were by Lionel Smith of Guaranty Sheet Metal and Roofing.

I had all chimneys tuck-pointed and waterproofed, and replaced missing chimney tops. The chimney top used is called Willows style.

Chimney top replaced and turret being worked on

Picture showing one missing chimney top and scaffolding to work on roof

Picture below shows chimney top replaced, turret repair finished, and new roof installed

Many types and sizes of chimney tops available. The Lady had the one called Willows.

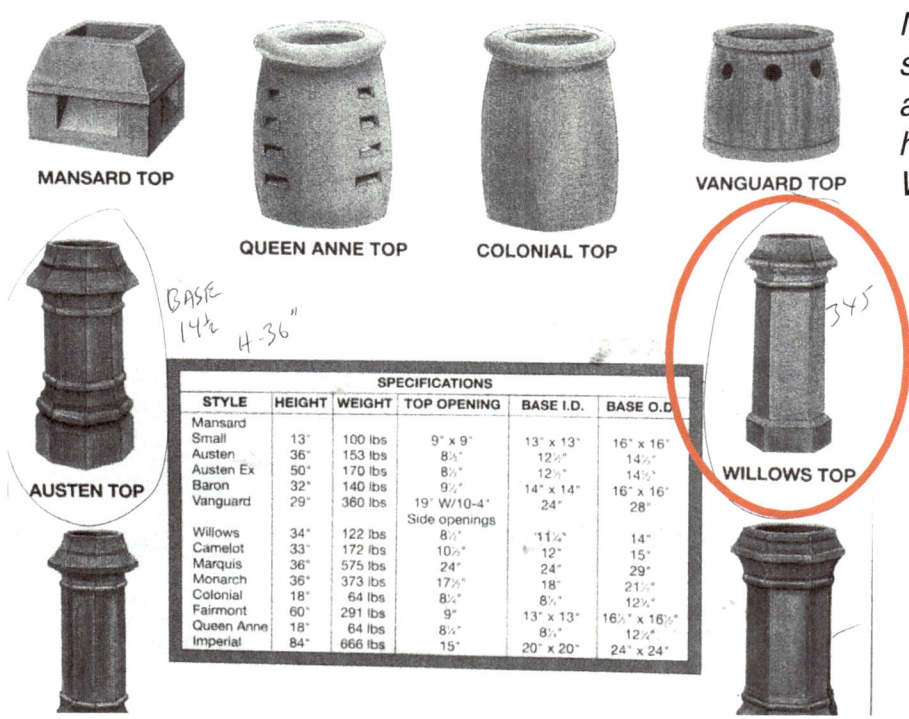

SPECIFICATIONS					
STYLE	HEIGHT	WEIGHT	TOP OPENING	BASE I.D.	BASE O.D.
Mansard Small	13"	100 lbs	9" x 9"	13" x 13"	16" x 16"
Austen	36"	153 lbs	8½"	12½"	14½"
Austen Ex	50"	170 lbs	8½"	12½"	14½"
Baron	32"	140 lbs	9½"	14" x 14"	16" x 16"
Vanguard	29"	360 lbs	19" W/10-4" Side openings	24"	28"
Willows	34"	122 lbs	8½"	11¼"	14"
Camelot	33"	172 lbs	10½"	12"	15"
Marquis	36"	575 lbs	24"	24"	29"
Monarch	36"	373 lbs	17½"	18"	21½"
Colonial	18"	64 lbs	8¼"	8½"	12½"
Fairmont	60"	291 lbs	9"	13" x 13"	16½" x 16½"
Queen Anne	18"	64 lbs	8½"	8½"	12¼"
Imperial	84"	666 lbs	15"	20" x 20"	24" x 24"

While the scaffold was up for the roof, I repaired the face of a dormer which was badly damaged. A small modern window and a vent for a heater were cut into the wooden pattern. These were to accommodate an apartment put in that space on the third floor.

This dormer was on the side of the house not visible from the street. The metal protecting the window was also badly damaged. I replaced it in copper. I added two small matching windows to give light to the dormer.

New Orleans Millworks, owned by Scott Taranto, specializes in historic architectural reproduction. Almost all the different specialized moldings needed for repairs were made by them.

Moldings made by New Orleans Millworks

Initial cost to Guaranty was $60,000.00 but ended up being $66,000.00 as I added other things. The full invoice (listed in Chapter 9.5) shows what materials Guaranty supplied and the work to be done. Materials included plywood sheeting, felt paper, copper nails, and copper for the valleys and to sheet two small flat roofs. I supplied the slate. Mr. Lionel Smith, owner of Guaranty Sheet Metal and Roofing, fabricated six copper roof vents as they were originally made.

The labor cost included removing the old slate roof, repairing any damaged roof, putting on plywood sheltering felt paper, and nailing on slate. They also step flashed the chimneys, replace the ridge tiles installed the 6 roof vents and sheeted two small flat roofs.

My roofers were from Guaranty. They were not only specialists with slate but also with copper. The copper gutters were made by Raymond Twickler but were installed by these guys from Guaranty.

Ronald "Ronnie" Hardy, Theodore "Teddy" Verdun, Vester "Red" Gray, Roland Hardy

A house at 8005-8007-8009 St. Charles has a turret on the roof with the same pattern of slate as the roof of The Lady. The rest of the roof probably had been replaced.

The house looks like it had been added to over the years

There are three addresses in tile embedded in the sidewalk in front of the house

Chapter 6
Part 3:
Gutters

The gutters and downspouts were originally made of galvanized metal and were badly damaged. I replaced them in copper.

Gutter with alligator

Sometimes a roof doesn't need a downspout but needs a way to shed the water. To do this, little copper open-ended tubes are built into the gutters. These open-ended tubes allow the water to go to ground. My workers called them "alligators."

The cost to install gutters and downspouts was $7,650.00.

Downspout replaced with copper

The gutter style used today is called K Style. Copper gutters used on The Lady were different. The difference in this style and the K gutter is the square bend part under the lip.

The gutters were made in their original style by Raymond Twickler. In Mr. Twickler's words, this style of gutter is called "ornamental gutters." He was the only one I found in the city that had the equipment to make this style.

The picture above is a K Style gutter. This and the half-round gutter are used today.

Copper gutter used on The Lady showing extra square bend under the lip.

Second floor gutters being replaced in copper, while the third floor gutters, still in galvanized metal, would be replaced next

Chapter 6
Part 4:
Cedar Scales

At the corner of The Lady was a turret style dormer. The copper metal roof of the dormer was approximately 17 feet tall with a circumference of approximately 25, or 31 feet when measured from the bottom curved edge. The circular part and sides of the dormer are covered in cedar shakes I call "scales."

Since the turret was the focal point of the house, I wanted to emphasize it. I also wanted to have harmony with the roof slate colors. The color I chose was Navajo Red, an Olympic solid stain. The sides of this dormer, the sides of the other dormers, and the front large dormer were covered in scales also. I decided to use a tan color for them called Chamois.

There are many profiles of cedar shakes, called fancy cuts. I could not find the profile I needed to match the one on The Lady.

I had a book on making jigs for special projects. I found instructions for a simple jig, which was just what I needed. I cut the correct profile from a profile called "round." I was able to use my band saw and the jig to cut the correct profile.

Round

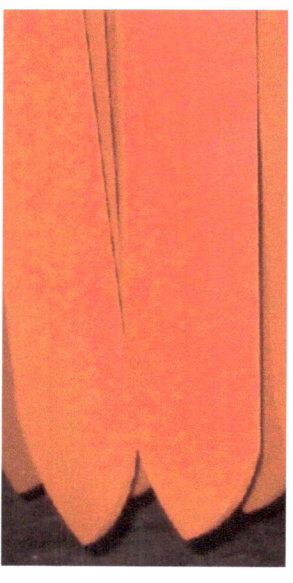
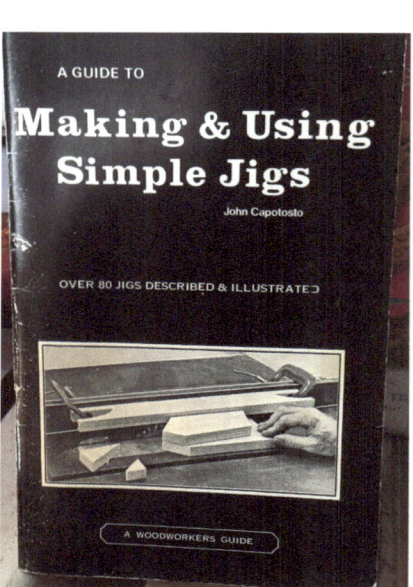

Profile of shake I needed

Simple jig to cut profile I needed

Chapter 6.4: Damage to Exterior: Cedar Scales

I wanted to get the best protection for the cedar wood, so I decided to dip them in stain.

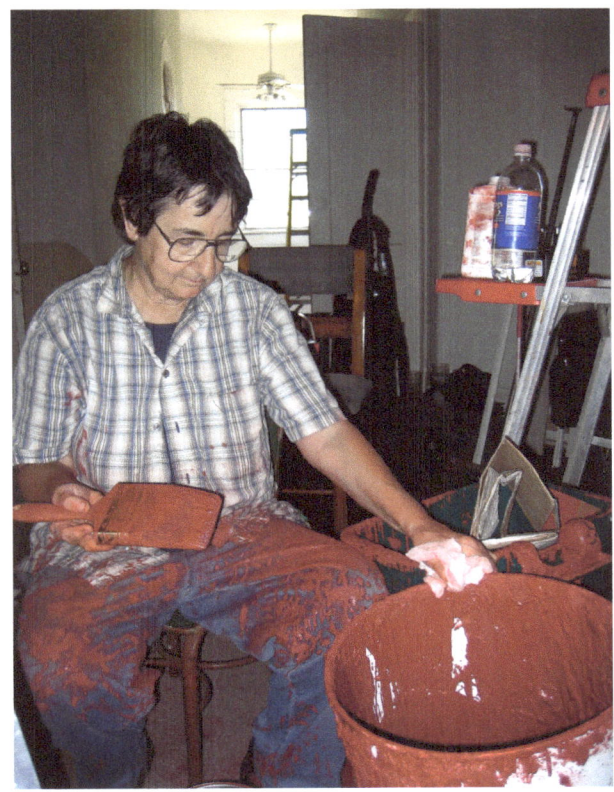
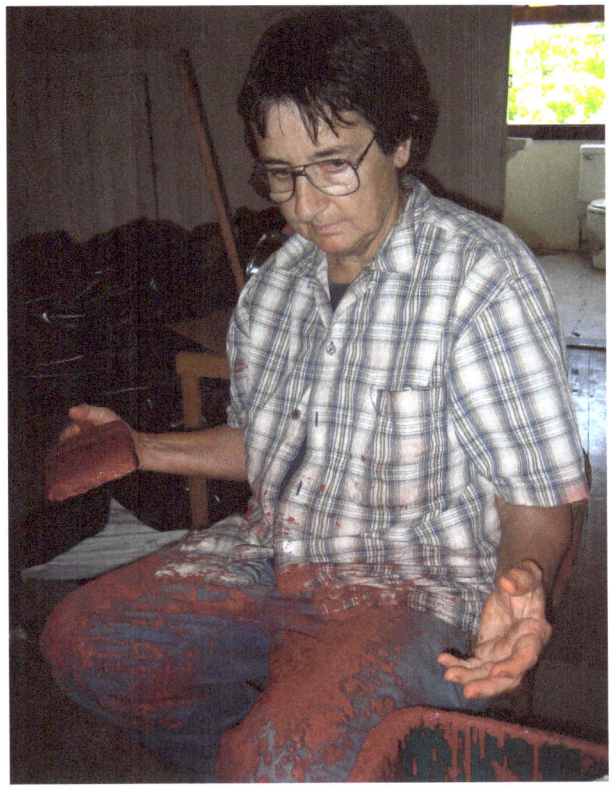

As you can see, I really put myself into my work.

The dormers had scales on their walls. One dormer, which was on the front of the house, had scales on the side wall and the front. On these scales, I used a tan Olympic oil stain called Chamois.

Dormer with scales on side wall

Felt used under scales

Scales on the front dormer

Chapter 6
Part 5:
Porch Support, Brickwork, and Grates

Chapter 6.5: Damage to Exterior:
Porch Support, Brickwork, and Grates

The porch's supporting brickwork and grates, as shown in the photo below, had fallen into disrepair and were in need of attention. This chapter will discuss the corrections made to these elements of the porch.

The bricks needed tuck-pointing. Tuck-pointing is the process of removing and replacing deteriorating mortar joints between bricks. The terms tuck-pointing and repointing are used interchangeably.

All but one of the grates had been stolen, and I replaced them with reproduction aluminum ones. I think the mold used was made from an original old grate.

The only original one left

Aluminum replacement

Chapter 6.5: Damage to Exterior:
Porch Support, Brickwork, and Grates

At some time, the original old grate was replaced with this small square one. It would later be removed and replaced with an original style grate.

Brickwork being repaired

Chapter 6.5: Damage to Exterior: Porch Support, Brickwork, and Grates

Brickwork repaired and grates replaced. The grates would later be painted black.

Chapter 6
Part 6:
Porch Floor

Chapter 6.6: Damage to Exterior: Porch Floor

The front porch was damaged, but in only one place. When it rained, I noticed water spurting out of a hole and the bottom of a square wooden box-like structure. This box ran from the floor to the ceiling and was attached to the porch wall. I removed one side of the box and saw a galvanized gutter downspout.

It seems someone had nailed a sign or something on the box structure and the nail had punctured the downspout, which was hidden in the box. When it rained, the water would spurt out of the hole and run onto the porch, causing the porch to deteriorate.

This picture shows the downspout replaced in copper.

After the downspout was replaced, it was re-covered as before.

Chapter 6.6: Damage to Exterior: Porch Floor

The other parts of the porch were also damaged in places.

Gulf Lumber Co., Mobile Ala. stamped on the back of one of the porch boards

In 1919, a part of the circular porch was taken to make a closet in Apartment B.

The picture shows how this was one thing that changed the outside symmetry of the house. The other being the removal of the first and second floor Marengo side railings.

Close-up picture shows the room was built over the original porch flooring

Chapter 6.6: Damage to Exterior: Porch Floor

Porch boards being removed as brickwork being repaired

The porch is circular so the floor boards were cut with a taper. This picture shows the tapers were random.

Removed the old floor boards and rebuilt and strengthened the floor support

Chapter 6.6: Damage to Exterior: Porch Floor

Support floor almost finished

Because the porch was circular, the porch boards were tapered. The porch boards were cut from old heart pine.

All of the porch floor tapers had to be calculated. This became more difficult as the circular porch transitioned into a straight porch. The tapers and the tongue and groove were cut in the front yard by Michael Hendrix.

Chapter 6.6: Damage to Exterior: Porch Floor

Fascia board being attached

Chapter 6.6: Damage to Exterior: Porch Floor

Ruby dog checking out the new floor

Porch floor boards being trimmed to length

Chapter 6
Part 7:
Porch Wall and Ceilings

Chapter 6.7: Damage to Exterior: Porch Wall and Ceilings

The porch ceiling is an unusual and beautiful work of design. It had been painted many times and was therefore hiding some of its structure. You could only barely see the beaded board, which was an important part of its design.

Part of the ceiling and turret wall in early stages of paint removal.

Later in the paint removal process, you could begin to see the beaded board and other design elements in more detail.

The hardest thing was to get the paint out of the bead of the beadboard ceiling.

Two types of boards used for walls, ceilings, and wainscoting are tongue and groove beadboard and V board.

We used heat guns, paint removers, and scrapers made for the job of removing the paint in crevices.

I wanted the ceiling and turret walls to show all of their detail.

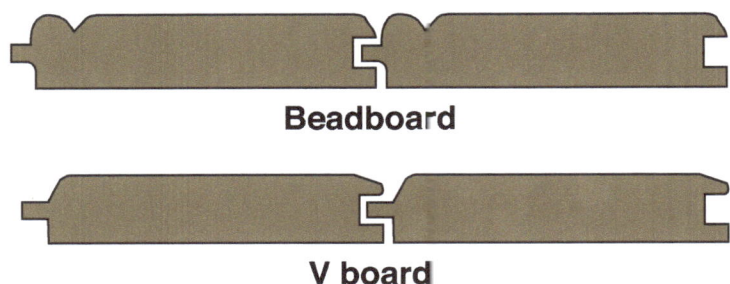

Beadboard

V board

Removing existing paint from walls

Sanded and final cleaning showing beautiful old cypress

Removing Paint on Second Floor Turret Walls and Ceiling

We used 2 x 4s and netting in order to protect Stanley Lee while working on the porch. He used ladders and scaffolding to work on the ceilings. As added protection, we put up a large black cat. This delighted some passing children who were heard to say, "That's not a cat, that's a puma!"

Chapter 6.7: Damage to Exterior: Porch Wall and Ceilings

Ceiling with paint removed and showing tape put on to begin painting the sections

First color was an oil stain called Navajo Red

The patterned slate roof colors influenced my decision to paint the ceiling and turret walls the way I did.

I wanted the ceiling and turret walls to show the detail. All the colors on the ceiling and turret walls were done in an oil solid stain. I believe an oil stain is absorbed into the wood and provides better protection. The red was an Olympic oil stain, but William Watts with Farrell Calhoun paints made the Chamois tan stain for me.

Second floor ceiling with black iron vents

I chose the color Navajo Red to be the main color of the turret walls, the same color used on the scales of the turret. The color scheme shows the turret as a continuous structure through all three floors.

Chapter 6.7: Damage to Exterior: Porch Wall and Ceilings

Turret in total, showing how the red color used does emphasize it as the dominant shape

Chapter 6
Part 8:
Porch Railings

Chapter 6.8: Damage to Exterior: Porch Railings

The porch railings were badly damaged.

Chapter 6.8: Damage to Exterior: Porch Railings

The posts that the railings were attached to had to be repaired. All railings and posts were repaired with old cypress.

Chapter 6.8: Damage to Exterior: Porch Railings

Old nails were removed, and parts replaced as needed

Chapter 6.8: Damage to Exterior: Porch Railings

Finished railing and columns

CHAPTER 7

Interesting Things About The Lady

Chapter 7: Interesting Things About The Lady

After I acquired The Lady, I started to explore the house by first going through all the attics. I found there were three levels of connecting attics. This proved useful when rewiring the second and third floor apartments.

The most exciting thing I found in one of the attics was the beveled glass front door. There were some broken pieces, so I suppose that was why it was in the attic. The person I bought the house from told me he wanted to keep it. I convinced him that I would have it repaired and that it belonged to the house.

Mr. Henry Lips, who was well known for his beveled glass doors, repaired it and reinforced the glass panel. Although it is only a single door and only half is beveled glass, he said that it was unusual because of the many circular glass pieces in the door and transom.

I also explored under the house. I saw all these really thin tubes coming down in a lot of different locations. I finally realized these were the remains of a voice speaker tube system. You could use these to talk to the cooks and perhaps to other people in the house. To talk, you would pull down the little handle, and the center would open up, allowing you to speak and be heard. The following explains just how effective the speaker tubes were: "Two persons standing at each end of a simple tin pipe, 1 inch in diameter, 50 to 100 feet or more long, with several elbows in it, and carried through a half a dozen rooms, can still converse quite readily in a low voice." (*Manufacturer and Builder*, Mar. 1872, p. 67)

Marked "PAT. JAN. 23, 1900"

By measuring under the house and then in the house, I found indentations in the walls near the doorways. I opened the wall indentations in these locations and found the tube's beginning.

I would find where the tube started in each apartment on the side of the door that opened to the hall. Then, I dropped a weighted string into the tube. Attached to the weighted strings, which ended up under the house, were little pieces of paper with the corresponding apartment number on them. Under the house, all of these pieces of paper flapped in the breeze. I wish I had a picture.

By doing this, the electrician was able to easily run wires through the walls. At this time, I put in an intercom and door release system. You can talk to someone who pushes your apartment button at the front door and also unlock the door.

Most all of the woodwork was painted white. When I removed the paint, I found these mother of pearl push buttons. They were on the inside and outside of the apartments' door frames. They had to be put in after 1919, as before then, there was no electricity in the house.

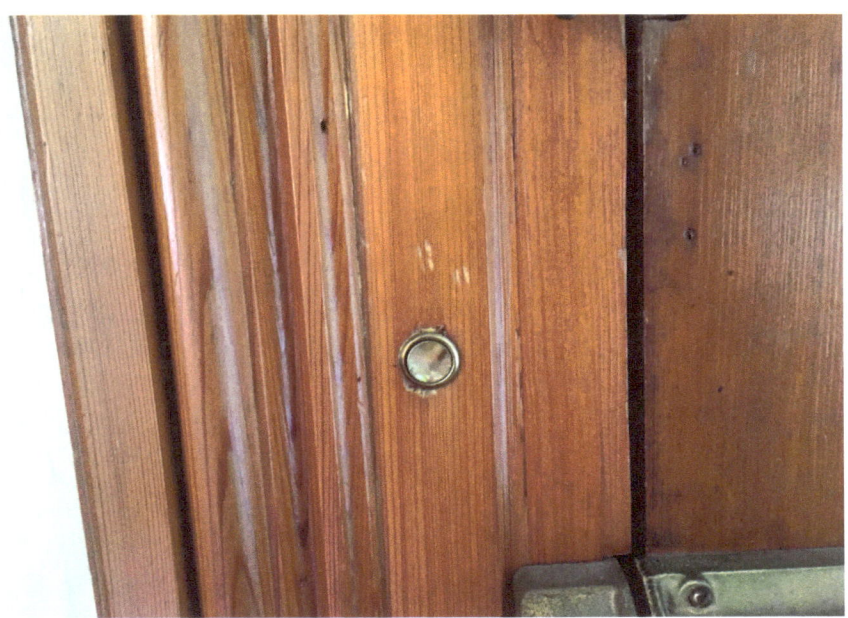

Inside apartment doorway. Maybe to call the manager?

Outside Apartment G entrance. I suppose the button outside the apartment was used to announce a visitor to the apartment.

The window and door casings have similar profile. This profile is cut into a single piece of cypress board. A casing is a frame around a window or a door. They would meet at a decorative corner block. There are many styles of these blocks, but the ones used in The Lady are rosette bullseye blocks. Blocks eliminate the need for complex mitering where casings would meet.

Plinth base blocks shown at far right. "Plinth" means lowest.

A block called a Plinth block is used where the casing ends. Door casings end at the floor but some window casings end at a window ledge. The Plinth block makes a neat transition with the base molding at the floor or window ledge.

On the first floor, the window and doorway casings are the same style. This style profile is cut into a single wide cypress board.

The second floor window and doorway casings are made of three different moldings put together to give the appearance of a wide casing.

Liberty Lumber is located at 5383 Tchoupitoulas Street in New Orleans. Liberty Lumber was (and may still be) owned by Mr. Thomas Hunting. I believe he owned it for some 35 years, but it has been there since 1923.

At one time Liberty had a large millshop. I needed some more casing molding, so I brought a sample to the millshop. Mr. Felix ran the millshop and could replicate anything that needed to be milled. He made the knives to match the sample and ran the molding that I needed.

Chapter 7: Interesting Things About The Lady

A transom is the horizontal piece that separates the door frame from the window above it. The transom window adds additional light to an area. Transom windows can be opened. Hot air rises and goes out the open transom window, then out the open front or back door transom windows. This air movement helps to ventilate and cool the house.

All of the doors leading to the hall and some inside an apartment have transom windows. There are transom windows over the front and back hall doors, which open to the outside. The Lady's transom windows are rectangular. There are other shapes used such as a fan shape over a fancy door.

The wood panels covering the bottom half of the walls of a room are called wainscoting. In what was the original dining room, there is wainscoting made of alternating strips of oak and mahogany with a mahogany top rail.

When I acquired The Lady, this wainscoting and most of the casings and baseboards had been painted. As I started to remove the white paint, I realized the surface painted over was originally shellac. Shellac seals the pores of wood so the paint did not penetrate the wood. This made it easier to remove the paint and reveal the beautiful wood underneath.

Chapter 7: Interesting Things About The Lady

Mrs. Estelle Flaspoller West mentions that the floors of The Lady were beautiful, wide pine. She also said the floors were always covered with rugs. I think the wide pine floor she mentions was the only floor. In other words, there was no subfloor. The rugs would be necessary because of the possible spaces between the floor boards causing drafts, moisture, and possibly insects.

I believe after the house was sold and changed into apartments, new floors were added over the original floor. The floors in the halls and all the rooms except for what was the kitchen, the first and second floor small side porches, and the third floor are all oak called "Philadelphia Strip." These are thin strips of oak surface nailed about every six inches. I believe this flooring was sold with the nail holes pre-drilled. These floors finish beautifully.

The hardwood floors after refinishing

An ad I found in a newspaper dated June 20, 1920, mentions that the apartment for rent had hardwood floors.

Wainscoting and Philadelphia Strip floor

Floor before refinishing. You can see it was surface nailed about every six inches.

On the second floor is a large room Mrs. West called the "sewing room." She said several times a year a seamstress would come and sew for the family.

The room is divided into two sections by a partial wall and ceiling with two large columns flanking the two small side walls.

The windows on the first and second floor facing Prytania and the windows on the second floor facing Marengo had wooden pull-up sunscreens.

There are three sunscreens for each window. One had movable slats which would allow you to adjust the amount of light you wanted. The other two had fixed slats.

Not all of the windows that originally had sunscreens still had them.

When we tried to pull the sunscreens up from their storage area, they would fall apart. We tried to duct tape the corners and gently pull them up but did not have much luck. The glue originally used to hold the sunscreens together was failing.

There are130 slats in the smallest sunscreen. Try as I might, I could not put even one sunscreen together.

I had reconciled myself to having no sunscreens on the windows. Then, I showed them to Joseph Silguero. He's the kind of guy who can do most anything—carpentry, plumbing, roofing, flooring, adding rooms, kitchen cabinets, etc. I showed him all the pieces and parts I had, including the one held together with duct tape and missing slats.

I now have eight sunscreens, thanks to Joseph. Below are pictures showing one with movable slats and one with fixed slats.

Sunscreen with adjustable slats

Sunscreen with fixed slats, showing exposed pull-ups. These were used to pull the window from under the window storage area.

On each side of the window were grooved trim boards. These grooves held the sunshades and allowed them to be placed at different heights.

There are two metal springs on only one side of the sunscreen. By pushing the window against the spring side you can move the sunshade up and down the grooved side boards. When you release the side pressure, the springs hold the sunscreens at the height you want.

When the sunscreens were not being used, they would be stored in the space below the window. When you wanted to use them, you opened a hinged panel and pulled them up to whatever height you wanted.

Above: Hinged panel covering storage space. Bottom right: Sunscreen inside storage space (viewed from above).

CHAPTER 8

A House and a Home

Chapter 8
Part 1:
The Flaspollers

Chapter 8.1: A House and a Home: The Flaspollers

The Lady exists because of the Flaspollers. The following is an overview of the Flaspoller family. More information on the family can be found in Chapter 9: Of Interest to Some.

Mr. and Mrs. Bernard H. Flaspoller made their money in the grocery business.

They had five children: three sons and two daughters. One son, Herman, died young at age 21. The other two sons, August and Henry, joined the family grocery business. They grew the business and it was very successful.

One of their daughters, Bertha, married William Drott. She later divorced and she and her two daughters went back to 4032 to live with her mother. She lived there and eventually owned part of The Lady until it was sold in 1919.

The other daughter, Caroline (Carrie), did not marry. She lived a life of privilege, partying, and traveling. She also did a lot of charity work. She inherited part of The Lady where she lived until she and Bertha sold it.

Mrs. Flaspoller and Henry got out of the grocery business. August remained and continued to expand the business, eventually bringing his sons on board.

Mrs. Flaspoller became very active in real estate. Henry was also involved in real estate but was active in the banking business as well.

When Mrs. Anna Flaspoller died in 1910, she left her children 4032 Prytania (The Lady) and eight other properties, which I believe were rental properties.

Chapter 8
Part 2:
Tenants Through the Years

Chapter 8.2: A House and a Home: Tenants Through the Years

The Lady was more a home than a house to its residents. To reach one's apartment, one first entered a communal hall in which there was a sense of not being alone. Three special residents made the house a home. Two lived in The Lady when I acquired her, and one moved in soon after. All lived in their apartments the rest of their lives.

The first original tenants were **the Browns**. Mr. Brown was retired from the cotton business. They were childless. To my knowledge, no one visited them. At their funerals, I learned they were related to U.S. Representative Lindy Boggs, who was in attendance.

My first Christmas in The Lady, I put a Christmas tree in the front hall and invited everyone to decorate it. The Browns eagerly participated (pictured below). The tenants enjoyed the company of the Browns at the tree trimmings and small barbeques I had in the back yard. Every year since, we have enjoyed the Christmas tree tradition.

The Browns with Anna Guidry

Mimi decorating the tree

The house residents and myself enjoying our annual Christmas tree decorating throughout the years. In the top photo, standing at far right, is another resident who was important to all in the house, Ms. Judith Almon.

Ms. Anna Guidry also made our house a home. She moved in soon after I acquired The Lady and stayed almost thirty years. She was a Cajun from Breaux Bridge and could really cook. She was a seamstress for a lingerie company and did tedious work for little pay.

Almost always, opening the front door to the main hall, one was greeted by wonderful aromas from Anna's kitchen. Many tenants went to Anna for cooking tips and help with sewing projects.

Anna Guidry made this amazing outfit from garment scraps from her seamstress job.

Lyle, a resident, wears the outfit one Mardi Gras. Ms. Anna Guidry is next to her.

When *The Lion King* was performed in New Orleans, the lead actor, **Fred Inkley**, stayed at The Lady as a favor to his cousin, a former tenant. We were excited to be invited to see him backstage.

The photos below show us watching him being made up and costumed and Anna trying on the lion's claw gloves.

When Ms. Guidry developed cancer, one or the other of us took her to her doctor's appointments and cancer treatments. She wanted to die in The Lady, her home, and she did. I was with her.

The Browns, Mrs. Almon, and Ms. Anna Guidry, I call residents because they lived in The Lady until the ends of their lives.

There were also some I call residents because they lived here for quite some time.

Mimi Landry, my first tenant, lived at 4032 for almost thirty years and then bought her own house.

Chapter 8.2: A House and a Home: Tenants Through the Years

My first tenant, **Mimi Landry**, shares her memories of The Lady:

As Best I Remember
by Mimi Landry

Forty years ago, when I was living in a nondescript apartment complex in Metairie, I called Arden Stewart about her ad in the Times-Picayune for an apartment on Prytania Street. When I arrived for a viewing, she opened the door to a quite large, freshly-painted room that was flooded with sunlight from all directions. (This space had been used as a storage attic for gowns and other Mardi Gras paraphernalia by the original occupants.) Now, if I were the lucky first caller, it would become my home! I was charmed by the two small bedrooms tucked into the eaves, a smaller kitchen, and an even smaller bathroom with beautiful colored glass windows. There was also a turret room with a view of Prytania Street rooftops where I imagined I could spend hours scrutinizing middle school writers' work. When I told Arden that I would love to rent the apartment, her response was, "Call me tomorrow." And call I did—numerous times, pleading that I was an employed teacher—respectable, quiet, well-mannered, and not at all as "silly" as she accused me of being when I practically begged, "Why can't I rent this apartment?" Arden finally relented, and I spent twenty most interesting years at 4032.

I baked cookies for the Browns, an elderly couple who resided downstairs by the front door, and they regaled me with stories about the city before the streets were paved. Miss Guidry became my pull-yourself-up-by-the-bootstraps counselor and seamstress, and I became her chauffeur. And...at the back of the house in a tiny room sat Miss Cropsy—the doorway wide open. We feared she might blow up the house because she smoked one cigarette after another with the gas burners on her stove flaming.

Over the years, apartments turned over, and a new crop of younger renters appeared. Norman, who moved into Miss G's apartment, escorted me to a couple of outrageous costume parties. Dr. Jim, upon graduating from medical school, crawled up the fire escape to celebrate with several cold ones, stretched out on his beach lounger, placed precariously on the slanted tin roof. Needless to say, his wife was not amused, and I felt I should be out there to monitor the situation—a sleepless night for me. And Scott and Arden—appropriately armed— played Keystone Kops one night, surrounding the house in search of a suspected burglar. How could I not be amused? Meanwhile, I had grown older and realized it was time to purchase my own home.

If you were to ask me where I grew up (a frequent question in New Orleans where one's lineage is of paramount importance), you might expect me to answer, "Why in Metairie and New Orleans, of course." But, in fact, I really grew up in my aerie at 4032 Prytania Street!

Frank Relle, a photographer born and raised in New Orleans, has lived in The Lady for seventeen years. He graduated in Cognitive Science and Philosophy from Tulane. His work is in the collections of the Smithsonian Museum of American History, the New Orleans Museum of Art, the Ogden Museum of Southern Art, the Museum of Fine Arts Houston, and in the private collections of Wynton Marsalis, Brad Pitt, Ellen DeGeneres, Drew Brees, and Sheryl Crow.

Todd Ritondaro has kept an apartment in The Lady for more than 10 years. Because he works in all aspects of the movie industry, he is not always here. Todd is a film writer/director and photographer who studied filmmaking at NYU's Tisch School of the Arts. He also hosts a podcast, Frame & Sequence, interviewing filmmakers, artists, photographers, and storytellers. He divides his time between New Orleans and Los Angeles, but can often be found, camera in hand, in small European towns.

Chapter 8.2: A House and a Home: Tenants Through the Years

Michelle Faucheux shares an apartment with Todd, both of whom have hectic family and work schedules. A native New Orleanian, she is a commercial producer and LA Times-published writer working on her first book about being a three-time Louisiana beauty queen. She splits her time between New Orleans, Los Angeles, traveling, and her mountain cabin with Todd and their book collection.

Margaret Morley was a resident but is now a friend. While renting a small apartment, she decided to change her life, went through law school while working full time, and passed the bar exam. She is intelligent and determined. She practices Family Law, which is less lucrative, because those she represents need her help.

Margaret shares her memories of The Lady:

My name is Margaret Morley. I moved to New Orleans in June of 1995 from New York City. I was about to turn 37. I sublet a place for two months at 1310 Marengo Street. It was across the street from a massive corner house with a turret: The Lady, a.k.a. The Stewart House. I fell in love with her on sight. She looked haunted. She needed a paint job but her distressed look only added to her charm and visions of ghosts. I saw people parking and going in and out and realized it wasn't just one person's home. I asked one of them if there were any available apartments. That was Mimi Landry, and she told me there was almost always an available apartment. She gave me Arden Stewart's phone number. In NYC this would be unheard of. No one ever gives out a person's number without getting their permission first; they take your number instead. This was one of the many relaxed Big Easy cultural differences I would learn to embrace in the years to come.

I called Arden Stewart. She said she had a small cottage available on the property. I met her, saw the cottage, and took it. It was like my own little house in The Lady's shadow. Sometimes a person thinks they are just making a mundane decision that has no meaning beyond the obvious: a place to live, a place to rent. Taking that cottage had repercussions for the rest of my life. You do not just rent a place at The Lady. It is not just a place to live. It is an experience. The other denizens were all very interesting and many were artsy and beyond my previous cultural experiences.

I soon learned that Arden Stewart is not just a landlady. Her curiosity about people and all manner of things is unparalleled in my life. She had been a shrimper, a medical technologist, a glass blower; she knew how to fix plumbing and electricity. She knew how to build things. She took a strong interest in me. When she learned that I was finishing my college degree at night at Loyola (yes, at 37 years old; I was a late bloomer), she took an even greater interest. She expressed approval and support for a person who "jerks themselves up" and does something with their life. I finished the last credits (combined with my existing ones from Hunter College of the City of New York) at the end of May 1996. I had been going to night school for over 11 years. I was done, finally! All I had to do now was work and have fun with all that New Orleans has to offer.

Arden Stewart wasn't having any of that. She was asking what I was going to do with my life now. I was stunned that anyone thought I should do more! Wasn't 11 years at night enough? And what would I do? She regularly questioned me: well, what do you like? What are your interests? I told her of my passion for justice, civil rights, and making life more fair for the poor and disenfranchised. I think I half-heartedly said, "Well, maybe I would like law school." But in truth, I hadn't one iota of belief that I could be a lawyer. Arden Stewart was like a dog with a bone and she pushed me hard. More importantly she kept telling me I could do it, that I was smart enough, that I could pass the classes. After about two years of her encouragement mixed with strong kicks in the butt, I applied to law school, won a scholarship to

Chapter 8.2: A House and a Home: Tenants Through the Years

Loyola Law School's night program, went to night law school for four years while working full time, graduated at the ripe old age of 45, and passed the Bar Exam on the first shot. I have been practicing poverty law for a non-profit in the family law area for over 16 years now.

I am sure of one thing: if I had not moved into the shadow of The Lady, if I had not met and been mentored and encouraged by Arden Stewart, I would never have ended up a lawyer. Funny how one decision can ultimately change the entire trajectory of a person's life.

Margaret recalls her first encounter with the numerous pets that called The Lady home:

I hadn't been living in the small cottage in the shadow of The Lady for very long, perhaps a month or two. One of the great things about living in the cottage was that it was set way back from the street with a large yard in front. It had high hedges so you couldn't see it from the street or find it if you didn't know it was there. It had its own gate up front and a winding path to the front door. None of the folks that lived in the big house had any need to come near the cottage so it was very private.

One day, happy to be home from work after a lovely streetcar ride, I opened the little gate to the cottage, and there in the grassy yard sat a massive dog—a Rottweiler! Well, I'd heard a thing or two about Rottweilers and felt a fast and furious pang of fear. I froze. The dog looked up at me quizzically but didn't bother to get up. I started to walk very slowly up the path, all the while trying to gauge any change in the dog's attitude. I saw the stub of a tail wagging, and the dog got up and started to walk toward me. I could tell for sure it wanted to be friendly. It came to me, and I petted its head, all the while not drawing a breath and just trying to negotiate my way past it and get into the cottage.

After I was in the cottage, back against the door, I resumed breathing.

I called Arden, and I'm sure she thought someone had been shot. A torrent of words flew from my mouth: "Arden! Arden! There is a dog in the yard! A big, big, big Rottweiler! Oh my god! How did it get there? Where did it come from? I thought I was going to die!"

Cool as a cucumber, she says, "Calm down, Margie. That's my dog. My vet called today and said he had a terrible rescue case, and I had to come see. The poor dog has been badly abused. Did you notice she only has three legs?" (Well of course I hadn't, as I was blind with fear and it was one of her back legs, so not immediately obvious to one in my state.)

Arden continued, "Dr. Zeller said I had to take her, that there was no one else for this dog. So, she's my dog, Margie. I think I'm going to name her Gita." She explained the name was a German word that means maybe "Girl" (my memory of that fails).

Stuff like this just doesn't go on in NYC, so my mind was blown. Just like that, Arden got a dog. Just like that, it's going to be living here, mostly on my side of the yard. Well, okay, so this is New Orleans. This is what it means to live in the shadow of The Lady. Anything can happen. Unexpected. Magical.

I came home every day to Gita in the yard for the next three years or so. She had shelter in rain or cold and was so happy to have a home. I had never had a pet in my life. She was the sweetest, gentlest, saddest-eyed dog you could imagine. I didn't know how incredibly a dog can convey love, curiosity, sadness, or guilt with their eyes and eyebrows and body language. Arden came home every afternoon and spent the rest of the night with Gita. Arden adored that Gita like nobody's business. A true love story for Arden, and a complete and happy revelation and education about dogs for me.

Gita had been living by the cottage for about two months. Arden was working hard to cheer her up. The abuse Gita had suffered showed, and she was quite sad. She didn't bark and didn't seem to know how to play. Arden's love was making some progress, but it was slow. There had been times when living at the cottage that I felt the grand Lady was really a presence more than an inanimate object. She looms over us and looks down on us, benevolently, for the most part, but curious too at the amazing amount of drama the various humans in the house had going on, buzzing here and there. And if she could, and the cause just, she'd help us out from time to time.

As if The Lady knew exactly what was needed, when I came home one day, there was Gita, but she was not alone. She was nose-to-nose with a short-legged, curly black-haired, tail-wagging dog. I was not as taken aback as when Gita showed up. I stopped in my tracks in some amount of awe and amazement. Again, I was reminded that living in the shadow of the grand old Lady really was magical. Anything might happen. The little black dog bounded over to me, jumping up and licking and loving on me. Gita struggled to her feet, wanting to follow the little dog's lead but just stood there once she was on her feet. She looked uncertain.

I called Arden when I got inside, and she explained that Jack had just appeared at the cottage gate. When she opened it, the happy little dog just walked into the yard as if it had always been

his home. Arden met the owner on crutches who was unsuccessfully trying to catch up to her runaway dog. She told Arden the dog's name was Jack, and she was having a hard time taking care of him because of her injury and her two other dogs! Arden told her she'd be happy to care for Jack while she recovered.

This was the beginning of a very happy period at the cottage. I came home to two dogs every day. Jack seemed to love me instantly, and that never hurts a person! Arden spent the evenings with both dogs. During the day, they had the run of the cottage side yard, and I would sit out with them in the early evenings. Within a few weeks, you could see incredible new life bubbling up in Gita. She tried to do anything Jack tried! By now, we were calling him Jackeroo or Jackarooney. He was definitely part of the family, and the owner had asked Arden to take Jack permanently!

One day, Arden called me with the incredible news that Gita was now barking right along with Jackeroo. He had taught Gita to find her voice along with her joy and joie de vivre! Both dogs were incredibly special and two of the many lovely creatures whose souls inhabit the grand Lady to this day.

Lyle Colombo lived in the house from 1993 until 2006. During that time, she left twice to spend the academic year in Berlin, Germany. She did graduate work in Berlin and wrote her doctoral dissertation on German philosophy there. After receiving her Ph.D from Tulane, she taught philosophy at Loyola University for several years. In 2006, she married and left 4032 to move in with her husband and start a family. She now spends her time developing a new career as a portrait painter.

Maura Hudsen—a resident and a friend. A tough Irish lady. Maura loves all animals and adopted a badly abused dog. As a young girl, she worked as a massage therapist for ten years on cruise ships. She visited 186 countries. Maura wanted to move to New Orleans. Her cousin, a former tenant, asked if I had an apartment available, and Maura moved into The Lady in 2007. She did massage therapy at the Roosevelt Hotel. She is also a good cook and loves baking. When the chef invited her to work in the kitchen, she gave it a try. Then, I retired from glass blowing, and she and I turned my studio into a commercial for-rent kitchen, Stepping Stone Kitchen—a place for young chefs to grow their skills. The pandemic slowed kitchen rental, and Maura resumed her other love, writing. She has published accounts of her experiences in many countries. She took a seductive picture of The Lady, which is this book's cover.

Sometimes a former tenant will pass by to say hello and share their current life. They still feel connected to The Lady.

Chapter 8
Part 3:
Is The Lady Haunted?

Chapter 8.3: A House and a Home: Is The Lady Haunted?

People always ask if the house is haunted. Whenever I ask a tenant if anything unusual happens in their apartment, they pause before answering. Then they tell of some little thing they see every now and then. Nobody seems very concerned. Maura Hudson says it best: "We are not alone."

I can only tell you what I observed in The Lady when I first acquired her. Sometimes when I got home at night I observed what looked like fog. We later laughingly would say, "It's foggy in the halls tonight." Mimi Landry, my first tenant, declared it a ghost and named it Victoria. We were more amused and accepting than frightened. I thought maybe it was the weather. One night, I came home and really thought the house was on fire. Aloud I said, "please stop," as it was scaring me.

I don't remember how long it was there or when it was gone. I suppose it just gradually disappeared, so we didn't notice. I was 29 at the time and had never owned a house before. This was not the nice double my father supposed I would buy.

This occurred where the front hall met the side hall and the stairway began. The hall ceiling is 14 feet high, and the fog was in the upper four feet. It extended partially up the steps and across the adjoining hall. It was easy to see through and had no scent. A picture of the area where the fog was is seen on the next page.

Upon entering the house, what we called a fog was visible above the picture molding and to the ceiling but not on the stairs. It appeared only at night, but not every night, and only on the first floor. Mimi named it "Victoria," and we sometimes said, "It's foggy in the halls tonight."

Another interesting event: Mr. Burke, an across-the-street neighbor, telephoned that there was smoke all around the turret roof. Was there a fire? There was no fire and no explanation. Mimi and I decided it was a cloud or perhaps the spirits leaving.

Mimi Landry, a former tenant from age 22 and a teacher at Country Day, also recalls unusual events:

I enjoyed dating and meeting friends and often returned about 10 p.m. One night, I unlocked the formidable front door and was puzzled by all the fog in the halls. It wasn't smoke, and I didn't think about it much until it appeared night after night.

On occasion when I struggled up and down the winding staircase with luggage, my cello, laundry, or groceries, a cold presence passed me, always in the opposite direction. Thus began the story of our resident ghost, Victoria, named by me. The first encounter alarmed me, but because she breezed by me multiple times, never harming me, I assumed Victoria had her reasons for roaming the halls, and they had nothing to do with me. In fact, I rather liked having her around! Victoria never appeared in my turret apartment, but many of the other residents—characters, all—did.

This is a picture from the newspaper of The Lady when she was sold in 1919. I examined the picture part-by-part for new information about her construction. To the left of the front entrance, I was startled to see what appeared to be someone looking out the bay window.

I don't know if the house is "haunted," but I agree with Maura who always says, "We are not alone."

CHAPTER 9

Of Interest to Some

Chapter 9
Part 1:
The Flaspoller Family

The Flaspoller Family

Bernard Henry Flaspoller —— **Anna Wilhelmina Potthorst**
- *Born in Germany in 1826*
- *Came to N.O. when 15*
- *Died August 4, 1886, at age 60*

- *Born in Salzaufler, Germany in 1840*
- *Died May 7, 1910, at age 70*

April 16, 1867, George Hawkins sold to Bernard H. Flaspoller Lots 5, 6, and 7 forming the corner of Prytania and Marengo for $1,350.00. This and half of Lot 4, which Mr. Flaspoller bought in 1884 for $210.00, is where The Lady was built in 1893.

An early map showed a large square building on lot 7.

The 1870 census listed four children and their parents, Anna (age 30) and Henry (age 31), living in dwelling number 68. The dwelling numbers in the census were not addresses but notations by the census taker of where he had been.

A fifth child, Herman, was born in 1873.

The city directory listed the Flaspollers' residence in 1873, 1874, and 1875 as "Marengo, corner Prytania."

I think the Flaspollers lived on Lot 7, Marengo corner Prytania, soon after purchasing the property in 1867.

Flaspoller Grocery Business

The Flaspollers owned and operated wholesale and retail grocery businesses.

Mrs. Anna Flaspoller was actively involved in running the grocery business with her husband. The city directory listed the addresses of the Flaspoller grocery stores in 1871, 1872, 1873, 1874, and 1875. From 1873 on, it also listed the Flaspoller residence as "Marengo corner Prytania."

Mr. Bernard H. Flaspoller died in 1886 when his sons August and Henry were 23 and 18, respectively. Then Mrs. Flaspoller and her older sons ran the grocery. The business was listed as B. H. Flaspoller Grocery, but August and Henry primarily ran it.

> *02/07/1898 Mrs. B. H. Flaspoller is retiring from the grocery business and has sold her interest to her two sons, August H. and Henry H. Flaspoller, which will be a co-partnership.*

By this time, Mrs. Flaspoller had built The Lady (1893) and was very involved in real estate.

By 1910, August and Henry were running, growing, and buying more property for B. H. Flaspoller and Son, known as one of the city's largest wholesale groceries.

On January 18, 1913, Henry H. Flaspoller sold all the grocery properties to August H. for $12,800.00 and dissolved the partnership. August H. brought in his son, August E., and renamed the business "August H. Flaspoller and Son."

By this time, they had greatly increased the value of their business.

> *11/23/1919 August H. Flaspoller continues to increase the value of the business. He buys adjoining property as a preliminary to modernizing and doubling its capacity. He bought twin buildings*

adjoining 316 Tchoupitoulas. Also owns 421 S. Peters... Two sons and three grandsons compose the firm... August H. Flaspoller president, Henry H. Flaspoller first vice-president, B. H. Flaspoller, manager of the city department, Sidney G. Flaspoller manager of country sales... Only outsider Charles H. Krammer secretary and treasurer.

August H. worked in the family business until his death in 1921.

Mrs. Anna Flaspoller

Mrs. Anna Wilhelmina Potthorst Flaspoller worked with her husband in the grocery business until he died in 1886. She continued in the grocery business, helped by her two sons, August and Henry.

She sold her interest in the grocery business to her two sons and turned her attention to real estate.

The following is an example of some of her real estate ventures:

On May 17, 1887, Mrs. Anna Flaspoller purchased property in Square 371, which is bounded by Prytania, Marengo, Pitt, and Constantinople. This square is directly across from Square 337 where The Lady was built. The property was 150 feet front on Prytania and 100 feet depth on Marengo. This was the corner directly across from The Lady. According to the tax records, 4035 on the corner of the 150 foot lot, existed in 1892. This was the house where her son August lived until he built his own house at 5308 Prytania. 4035 was built on a lot size a little over 67 feet. Mrs. Anna Flaspoller built a double on the remaining 82.7 feet. This became 4025/27 Prytania. Below is an ad in 1899 to rent 4025.

Chapter 9.1: Of Interest to Some: The Flaspoller Family

11/18/1899 FOR RENT 4025 Prytania St. near Marengo; downtown side of two story, double house; five large bedrooms, linen closet, parlor, library, large dining room, and large hall in center of house; all newly painted and papered; modern conveniences; outhouse and shed; Also house of same description No. 1424 Marengo, corner Perrier between St. Charles and Prytania. Apply 4032 Prytania.

I wondered where Mrs. Anna Flaspoller lived while The Lady was being built. In 1891, she was still living in a house on the corner of Prytania and Marengo. This was where, in 1893, The Lady was built. Since 4035, across the street on Prytania, existed in 1892, she could have lived there. Maybe she built it for that purpose. When she died in 1910, she still owned 4035. It seems she kept the houses she built to use as rental properties.

Mrs. B. H. Flaspoller

The unexpected death of Mrs. B. H. Flaspoller yesterday forenoon at her home, on Prytania and Marengo Streets, caused much genuine sorrow among her numerous friends throughout the city. Mrs. Flaspoller, though advanced in years, was a woman of remarkable vigor, and was an active worker of St. George's Episcopal Church, of the German Protestant Orphan Asylum and of the German Home for the Aged and Infirm.

She was a member of the board of managers of both the last named institutions for many years, and was the treasurer of the German Home since its organization, twenty-five years ago. Her presence and help will be greatly missed by these organizations and the many other worthy causes she so generously assisted.

She leaves to mourn her two sons, August H. and Henry Flaspoller, of the wholesale grocery firm of B. H. Flaspoller's Sons, founded by her husband and herself more than fifty years ago. She also leaves two daughters, Mrs. B. F. Drott and Miss Carrie Flaspoller, numerous grandchildren and a great-grandchild.

The funeral will take place this afternoon at 4 o'clock and Rev. Byron Holley, of St. George's, will officiate.

The cause of Mrs. Flaspoller's death is not revealed in this newspaper account:

Mrs. Henry H. Flaspoller arrived last evening from Covington, La., called here by the sudden death of her mother-in-law, Mrs. B. H. Flaspoller, who passed away yesterday, after three days of intense suffering.

Mrs. Anna Flaspoller left everything to her four living children, Herman having died earlier.

The property listed in Mrs. Anna Flaspoller's succession consisted of The Lady and eight other pieces of property. Each of her children took two pieces of the eight but co-owned The Lady.

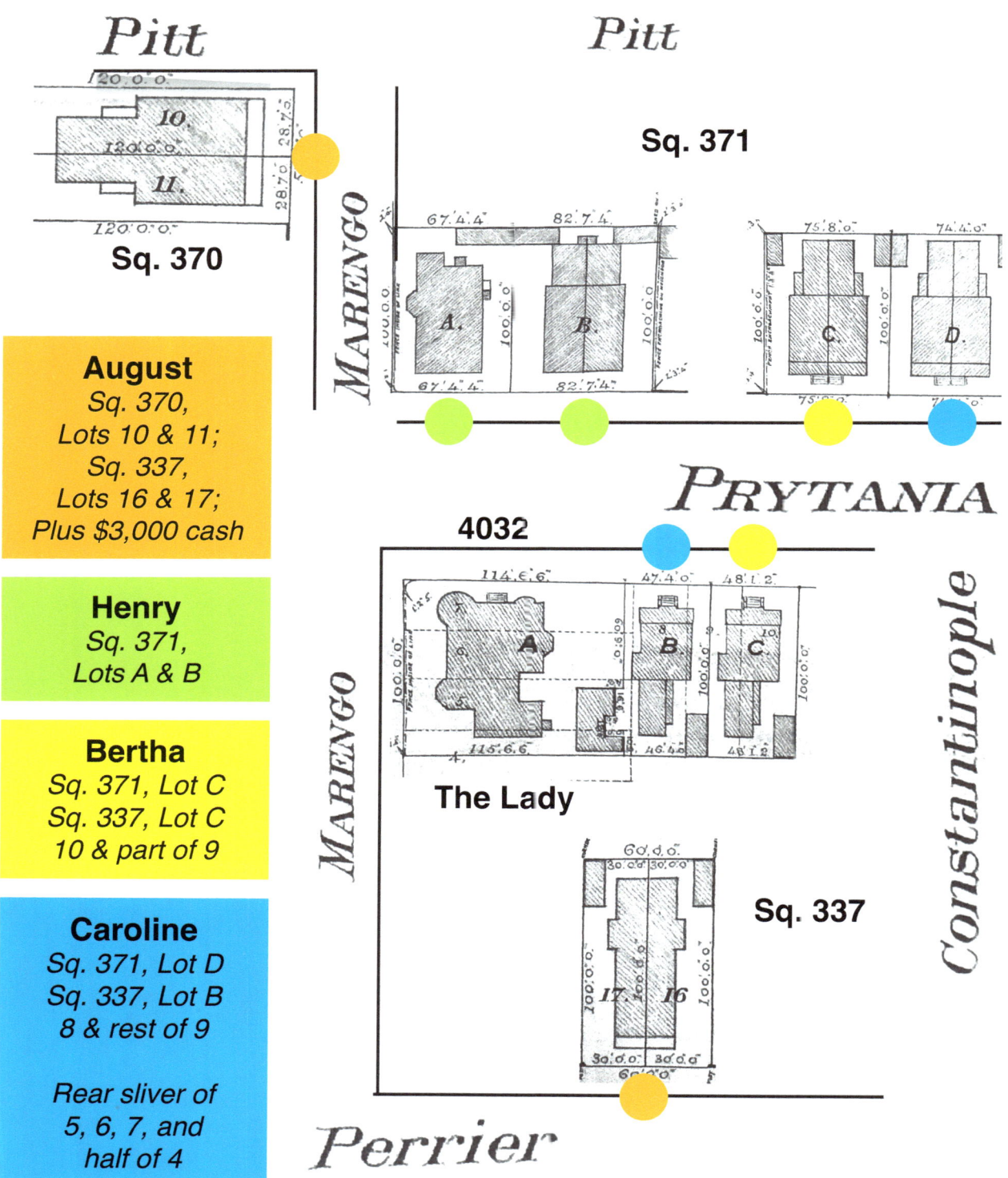

August H. Flaspoller

September 1884, August H. Flaspoller married Catherine Georgiana Weiss. In 1891, August was living at the corner of Prytania and Marengo. In the census of 1900, he and his wife and four children were living at 4035 Prytania, right across from The Lady. As required by the census, he stated he rented the property. His mother Anna had purchased the property in 1887 and built the house in 1892. Because he had four children, he probably moved in as soon as possible.

According to the census of 1900, his children were: Katie A., age 14, born in 1886; Gertrude Louise, age 13, born in 1887; August E., age 11, born in 1891; and Sydney, age 7, born in 1893.

On July 3, 1899, August Flaspoller purchased a piece of property further up on Prytania Street. It was described as half the square number 351 bounded by Valmont, Perrier, Leontine, and Prytania and measuring 200 and 1 feet and 10 inches front on Valmont and 100 and 39 feet and 4 lines front on Perrier Street. The price paid was $6,000.00.

An ad on April 8, 1900, for the other half of the square number 351 says Mr. Flaspoller is erecting a costly and elegant residence on the other half square number 351. This would be his house at 5308 Prytania St.

State tax records indicate the house was built in 1900, had fourteen rooms, eight bedrooms, wood frame construction, and a total of 6,420 square feet. Property taxes doubled from 1890 to 1891.

August H.'s main interest was the wholesale grocery business, but he was also involved in banking and the Krewe of Rex. In 1897, he was on the board of directors of the Provident Savings Bank. In 1913, 1914, and 1916, he was one of the directors of the Metropolitan Bank. On March 1, 1911, August H., referred to as the Duke of Groceries, was on the floor committee of the Rex Ball. The queen that year was Miss Rose Brice West, granddaughter of Judge A. G. Brice. The ball was in the palace at the Athenaeum.

DIED AUGUST H. FLASPOLLER - 6/4/1921 - age 68, died after an illness of 6 weeks, funeral will be at his residence 5308 Prytania and will be in the family tomb in Metairie Cemetery. Survived by three sons, August E., Bernard H. and Sidney G., a daughter Mrs. A. F. Commagere, one brother Henry H. Flaspoller and two sisters, Miss Caroline Flaspoller and Mrs. Bertha Flaspoller Drott, and 7 grandchildren.

6/16/1921 Wedding of Miss Lombard (debutante two years ago) and Mr. Tuttle Flaspoller. Owing to the recent mourning in the Flaspoller family only family members attended the June 15th wedding (death of August H. Flaspoller 6/5/1921).

Henry H. Flaspoller

Henry H. Flaspoller married Margaret Emma Tuttle on June 18, 1896. They had two surviving children: Bernard Tuttle Flaspoller, born 1897, and Margaret Estelle Flaspoller, born 1899. They are pictured outside the yard of The Lady. Estelle told Lee what she recalled of The Lady.

According to the 1900 census, Henry H. Flaspoller rented 4013 Prytania from his mother, Anna Flaspoller. Henry H., his wife, Margie, age 25, his son Bernard, age 3, and his daughter Margaret lived there.

Henry was in the grocery business with his brother August but sold his interest to August in 1913. While in the grocery business, he was involved with real estate.

Henry H. Flaspoller lived at 4941 St. Charles, in the house shown at right. He sold it in 1908. The newspaper article of the sale stated that the house was built in 1906.

I took this picture in 2019. The exterior looks the same as it did when sold by Henry H. Flaspoller in 1908.

Chapter 9.1: Of Interest to Some: The Flaspoller Family

In 1908, Henry H. Flaspoller sold his house at 4941 St. Charles and moved to Covington, LA.

07/19/1908 Mr. and Mrs. Henry H. Flaspoller who are making their home in Covington for the benefit of the latter's health spent part of last week in the city at the home of Mrs. B. H. Flaspoller.

According to the 1920 census, Henry H. Flaspoller lived at 1229 State St. Two newspaper clippings below state his address in 1912 and 1913.

10/27/1912 H. H. Flaspoller 1229 State arrested for speeding on St. Charles.

01/24/1913 Henry B.* Flaspoller of No. 1229 State St., received affidavits for speeding on St. Charles Ave.
*should have been Henry H.

Henry H. was an avid supporter of a military draft to obtain U. S. troops for World War I.

04/06/1917 Members of the Pickwick Club proclaim their allegiance and support of the President of the United States as a crisis of war exists between US and Germany. This resolution was seconded by H. H. Flaspoller who said his father had left Germany when he was 16 years and when he reached the age of majority had become an American citizen and a Democrat.

He said he stressed to his children and their children that they were free citizens of free America and that this was the noblest heritage he could leave them.

01/13/1922 Henry H. Flaspoller to succeed James H. Tharp as president of Liberty Bank and Trust.

The 1930 census shows Henry back in Covington with his wife. He was 62 and Margie E. was 56.

The following pages on his debutante daughter Estelle and his son Tuttle show evidence of his wealth and lifestyle.

Margaret Estelle Flaspoller

The caption of the article reads: "Think I've seen her at every Yacht Club dance this season. And between times on the links at the Country Club."

Estelle is the granddaughter who shared so much first-hand information on The Lady.

Margaret Estelle Flaspoller was constantly found in the society pages of the local paper. She was a debutante and a graduate of Isidore Newman School in New Orleans.

Estelle's father, Henry H. Flaspoller, hosted many parties and events in honor of his debutante daughter.

Chapter 9.1: Of Interest to Some: The Flaspoller Family

The following newspaper articles illustrate the Flaspollers' lifestyle of international travel and elite schools.

05/04/1913 - Mr. and Mrs. Henry Herman and their son and daughter will leave in June for a year or more in Europe.

7/18/1913 - Mrs. B. Flaspoller Drott, Miss Carrie Flaspoller, and Miss Violet Drott, and Miss Marion Coates, after a recent visit to London, are now in Paris, then Switzerland, Lucerene and Geneva, then Italy.

8/19/1913 - Mr. and Mrs. Henry Herman Flaspoller and their son and daughter, Tuttle and Estelle, both popular members in junior social circles, will travel to New York, then sail for Germany. They will go to Dresden, where Tuttle and Estelle will enter school for the season. Mr. Flaspoller will return to New Orleans for a short stay and return with Mrs. Flaspoller's mother, Mrs. James Smith Tuttle, who will visit on the continent with them and then be in Europe for a long stay.

2/27/1914 - Miss Estelle Tuttle Flaspoller skiing with school mates in Oberhof, Germany, with her parents Mr. and Mrs. Henry Herman Flaspoller and brother Tuttle for the holidays.

5/9/1915 - Miss Estelle Flaspoller, a student at National Cathedral School on the outskirts of Washington, has been so seriously ill her parents were summoned to her bedside.

5/25/1915 - Miss Estelle Flaspoller, who is recovering from a serious illness, will be in Covington for an extended period.

Estelle married William Alice West, Jr. in 1923. They had two children, Margaret (Margie) Emma and Blake Roger.

Her son Roger Blake became a judge. I met him and his wife Tilly when they visited the house. My research revealed he died the next year, 1987.

Judge Blake West, Son of Estelle Flaspoller West

I was honored to meet Judge West and his wife when they visited The Lady at my invitation. I also want New Orleanians to know he struck a blow for free speech and our Jackson Square musicians.

Born in New Orleans, Louisiana, Blake West earned a Bachelor of Arts degree from Tulane University in 1949 and a Bachelor of Law from Tulane University Law School in 1951. He was in private practice in New Orleans from 1951 to 1971.

On April 14, 1971, West was nominated by President Richard Nixon to a new seat on the United States District Court for the Eastern District of Louisiana created by 84 Stat. 294. He was confirmed by the United States Senate on June 18, 1971, and received his commission on June 22, 1971. West served in that capacity until his death on January 24, 1978.

In the late 1970's, Judge West presided over a case filed on behalf of street musicians who had been banned from parts of the French Quarter. The defense argued that the ordinance against the musicians was unconstitutional because it denied them free exercise of speech through their playing of music. Judge West agreed and issued an injunction blocking enforcement of the ordinance. This ordinance was the first to protect music as a form of free speech.

Judge Blake West was born May 10, 1928. He married Willey-Gayle Martin on September 26, 1953. Their children were: Melissa Gayle, Anne Estelle, Willey-Gayle Blake, and George Sebastian. Judge West died January 24,1978, at age 49.

Bertha and Caroline Flaspoller

Bertha married William Drott in 1881, but they later divorced. The 1900 census shows that she and her two daughters, Bertha and Violet, were living at 4032 Prytania. Her daughter Bertha married John Robinson Conniff on November 29, 1905 at St. George's Church. The reception was held at 4032 Prytania St.

The 1910 census had Bertha, Carrie, and Violet living at Peoples Avenue suburb in the 8th ward.

The 1920 census listed Bertha, Carrie, and Violet at 4013 Prytania, property that Bertha had inherited from her mother Anna. The 1940 census has Bertha, 79, and Carrie, 74, renting 507 Napoleon Ave., Apt. 2. Bertha died in October 1945 at age 84. Carrie never married, but the newspapers indicate that she often partied and frequently traveled. She died in 1947 at age 81.

Chapter 9
Part 2:
Costs

Dome Roof Work

Renaissance Roofing • Metairie, LA
June 7, 2007

Scope of work:
- Erect scaffolding around entire perimeter of dome roof to ensure safe work environment.
- Carefully remove 2 courses of existing slate parallel to dome and save for reinstallation later.
- Remove existing metal from entire dome down to wood deck.
- Replace wood decking, as needed (this work to be done at an additional $6.75 per sq. ft.)
- All unforeseen, hidden, structural-framing replacement with be completed on a time, ($75.00 per man hour) and material basis.
- Furnish and install new W.R. Grace ice and water shield underlayment over entire dome roof area.
- Furnish and install new red rosin "slip-sheet" over entire dome roof area.
- Furnish and install new 16 oz. copper flat seam interlocking roof panels for entire dome roof area (to match existing) including custom perimeter.
- Clean up and remove all debris created by our work from the job site.

The above work to be completed for the sum of $13,926.00.

Slate

Evergreen Slate Co., Inc. • Vermont Roofing Slate
March 24, 1999

All Vermont Roofing Slates to be 1/4" Thickness, Punched for Nail Holes, Palletized and Delivered by Flatbed Truck to the job site for customer unloading.

Qty	Description	Price	Total
50	14" x 10" Color mix: 6% Unfading Red 47% Unfading Green 47% Vermont Black	@ $479/sqr.	$23,950.00
		Total	$23,950.00

Scaffolding

United Scaffolding • LaPlace, LA
March 26, 2003

- Cost to put up and take down scaffolding: $3,624.00
- Rental of scaffold material: $600.00
- Rental of scaffold material 4/12/03 through 7/20/03: $2,227.68

Total cost to scaffold: $6,451.68

Roof Caps

C.C. & W. Enterprises, Inc. • Baton Rouge, LA
May 13, 2003

Qty	Description	Price	Total
8	Salv. Ridge (Decorative)	$15.00	$120.00
		Tax	$10.80
		Total	**$130.80**

DMS Trading • Carrollton, TX
July 31, 2003

Qty	Description	Price	Total
2	Misc. Clay Finial	$25.00	$50.00
	Freight		$95.00
		Total	**$145.00**

Willows

C.C. & W. Enterprises, Inc. • Baton Rouge, LA
May 13, 2003

Qty	Description	Price	Total
2	Willows Chimney Tops	$344.00	$688.00
	LTL Packaging		$55.00
	Freight		$150.00
		Tax	$27.52
		Total	**$920.52**

Gutters

Guaranty Sheet Metal Works, Inc. • Kenner, LA
May 2, 2007

Description	Amount
• To install 60' of copper gutter on top.	$5,600.00
• To install 70' of copper gutter on bottom.	
• To supply and install 60' of 4" round copper downpipe.	
EXTRAS:	
• To install copper gutter on circular front left bay window with 2 spigots.	$1,000.00
• To fabricate and install one copper door pan, hood and ledge flashing.	$750.00
• To install gutter on top yard side with miter and spigot.	$300.00

Total $7,650.00

Roof Work

Guaranty Sheet Metal Works, Inc. • Kenner, LA
March 27, 2003

Description	Amount
Draw #1	$12,000.00

- To remove the existing slate roof from the right side and front of the main house.
- To supply and install a treated 5/8" "cdx" plywood.
- To supply and install 30 pound U.L. rated felt.

Total $12,000.00

Guaranty Sheet Metal Works, Inc. • Kenner, LA
April 30, 2003

Description	Amount
Draw #2	$20,000.00

- To install slate roofing on the right and front side of the house in the pattern.
- To stage the roof and begin removing the left side.
- Once we get a count on the deliveries from Roofing Products, who are billing me directly for some reason, the amount of the copper sheets and our copper work, I will give you a detailed billing. I also faxed over the United Scaffolding bills I have paid.

Total $20,000.00

Guaranty Sheet Metal Works, Inc. • Kenner, LA
June 11, 2003

Description **Amount**

Draw #3 $66,000.00

- To install 10 x 14" slate roofing owner provided in the pattern requested with copper nails.
- To fabricate and install 16 oz. copper dormer, step, chimney, apron, window, drop edge, ledge, front and dormer and sill and small door hood.
- To fabricate and install copper flat lock roofs in two areas.
- To fabricate and install six copper decorative ventilators.
- To install copper gutters with new straps and stages.
- To replace 190' of treated 1 x 8" wood.
- To install 5/8" treated plywood and 30 lb. U.L. rated felt.
- To install ridge tile in cement.
- To pay the delivery fees from Roofing Products.
- To pay the bill for 27 sheets of 4 x 10' copper.

Amount paid through draws to date $32,000.00. -$32,000.00

Total $34,000.00

Chapter 9
Part 3:
Workmen Helped Save The Lady

Workers on Prytania

Over the years, I have had many repairs done by many different repairmen. I will list some who worked on The Lady more than a few times.

When I would have someone do a repair, they would see the amount of things obviously needing repair and become overwhelmed. I was constantly telling them to only concentrate on the one thing I was asking them to repair.

I would repair something when I had the money. I would stay and watch and ask questions. I learned a lot about all different kinds of repairs including sheetrock, carpentry, roofing, and plumbing.

Carpenters

One of my first carpenters was Phil Howard. He worked on repairing porch railings and did miscellaneous repairs. The thing I remember most was when he decided to repaint the metal turret. He went into the third floor attic and made his way to the turret. There was a primitive ladder which enabled you to climb up to the top of the inside of the turret. He then attached a rope inside the turret and dropped it to the outside of the turret. Then he built what he called a captain's chair and attached it to the rope. He got into this chair and swung around the turret, painting it. He was fearless.

Another incredible carpenter was Richard Stafford. He reattached some of the cedar shakes on the turret and also repaired and rebuilt some of the exterior gingerbread. The most impressive thing was making the curved sashes for the curved glass windows.

Mr. Steve Rome was a wood turner who made the mahogany balusters that were missing in the stairway. He was the first president of the Bayou Woodturners Club and was a skilled furniture maker. He also did some work that was needed to install the curved windows and sashes.

Loyd Alfonse Rodrigue (Junior) and Donald Morrison were carpenters who worked for Rogers Construction. They replaced the back siding with Hardie board. They replaced some quoins on the front wall edge, built a utility box for the electric meters, and took care of a few other small repairs which helped me a lot.

Angelo La Martina, Neri Menchu, and a crew of painters of Caeser Cruz put up the scaffolding needed to replace and paint the gingerbread on and above the first and second floor porches.

Michael Hendrix and his helper Carl Davis ("Bones") worked on repairing The Lady. Michael is a rough-in carpenter, a finish carpenter, and a cabinet and furniture maker. He knows all aspects of a complete renovation.

Cecil Travis Bennett (called "CT") was a contractor, but he usually worked right alongside his men. He and his men worked on The Lady off-and-on when I had any money. He would patiently show me how things were done from carpentry to flooring, painting sheetrock, etc. I considered him a friend.

His main carpenter was a Cajun named Woodreau Billot. Woodreau was born on a shrimp boat. His mother went back to picking shrimp three hours after he was born, so the story goes. He could not read or write. CT taught him how to sign his name so he could cash his checks. He spoke a kind of Cajun English. It took me a while, but I could finally talk with him. He drank two Dixie beers every day for lunch. He worked mainly in "cypree," as he called it. He was an amazing carpenter who could understand what you wanted and do it flawlessly. He confiscated a long piece of cypress I had, saying he needed it for a push pole. In the swamp, the water is shallow and you get around on a flat boat. You propelled the boat with a pole called a push pole. You put in the water and pushed, moving the boat along. He was related to a local called "Alligator Annie," which impressed me greatly.

There were a number of CT's painters who worked on The Lady throughout the years. The one I remember the most was Robert Bowie, who was called "Boo Boo." He taught me a lot about the different kinds of paints and when and where to use them.

Some of his other men who painted on The Lady were Harold Coates, Jessie Harrison, and Jack Simmons.

Frankie Penton, James Lee Osley (called "George") and Herman "Buddy" Beasley did sheetrock, carpentry, welding, and plumbing. Herman "Buddy" Beasley also repaired automobiles and trucks and rebuilt race cars. He kept my old truck running. They could do almost anything. They became friends and were very special to me.

Kirk Vallory is a wonderful carpenter but also a contractor. He knows everything about doing a complete renovation. It was hard to hire him for any of my repairs, as he had many clients in the French Quarter who kept him busy. Even so, if I had a special problem he would always come and help.

Plumbers & Electricians

My first plumbers were Alvin and Melvin Munch of Charles J. Munch and Sons. I hung around to learn whenever they did repairs like replacing and repairing faucets and even how to reinstall a toilet. I learned about the different types of washers, what a wax ring was, and more. At that time they were still repairing cast iron drains with oakum and lead. The most important thing they did for me was finding where the hot water circulating system had been disconnected and reconnecting it. This repair allowed hot water to be immediately available to all apartments no matter how far away they were from the hot water heater.

I now use Al Bourgeois Plumbers, a family-run plumbing business with a history of three generations of plumbers. Al Bourgeois started the business; his son Carl now runs it. One of his sons, Brad, and a cousin, Chip Trosclair, and Chip's mother Patsy now help run the business. Some of the plumbers have been with Bourgeois for years.

One I know well is Greg Dimarco and his son Chris. Greg knows everything about plumbing, from pipes to installation. I call him whenever I have a plumbing question or concern and he will come to the location and solve the problem.

When I call to schedule a service the phone may be answered by any of the above, but also by Jennifer Prejean. She is not of the Bourgeois family, but knows the business well.

My first electrician was Margiotta Electric. V. J. Margiotta started the company in 1910. His son, A. J. Margiotta was who I knew best. He was not only a great electrician, but also a good man who did a lot of charity work for small churches. His three sons, Vincent, Lawrence ("Larry"), and Joseph now run the business. I knew Vincent best, but lost touch when he started doing mainly the commercial work of the company. They are all fine electricians and good people.

Roofers, Sheetrock, Plaster, & Brick

My first roofer was Rudolph Schaff. He replaced slates that had slipped or were damaged. He worked on trying to keep the roof watertight

Chapter 9.3: Of Interest to Some: Workmen Helped Save The Lady

until 2003, when I was able to replace the roof. He also replaced some metal flat roofs. He taught me what a standing seam roof was and let me help to put one on. He also welded a trellis which arches over the sidewalk entrance to the side yard. It is now support for my Confederate Jasmine. He also worked in copper and put the copper gutters on the Cottage. I got to know him well and called him a friend.

Guaranty Sheet Metal and Roofing was started by Lionel Smith in 1970. He grew his company into a full-service sheet metal and roofing company. He brought his son Lonnie into the business and grew it even more. Their crew of roofers, experienced in working with slate, replaced my historic patterned slate roof. Mr. Lionel Smith rebuilt all the original roof vents just as they were, but in copper. His roofers Ronald "Ronnie" Hardy, Theodore "Teddy" Veruden, Vester "Red" Gray, and Roland Hardy did the slate roof attached all the copper gutters.

Sheetrock repairs were done by CT Bennet's worker Frankie Penton. Now all my sheetrock is done by Gerald Colopy.

Jose and Josa Rosa did the hall repairs with hot mud plaster.

Brick work was completed by Lawrence Prosper, Lee Vernon, and Teddy Pierre.

New Orleans Millworks, owned by Scott Taranto, specializes in historic architectural reproduction. Almost all the different specialized moldings were made by them.

Stanley Lee has worked for me since 2013 and although he considers himself mainly a painter I soon found out he was much more. He can hang and refinish sheetrock and repair ornate plaster moldings. He knows basic plumbing and a fair amount of carpentry.

www.ingramcontent.com/pod-product-compliance
Lightning Source LLC
Chambersburg PA
CBHW041423010526
44119CB00015B/352